# When the Barbarians Came

By

Don Taylor

First Writes Publications London 1995

First Writes Publications, London 1995


First Writes Publications are published by
First Writes Theatre Company Ltd
46 Maldon Road Acton W3 6SZ


Printed by UTL Printing, 38 Langham Street, London W1N 5RH


© Don Taylor 1995

ISBN 0 9524159 3 3

This play is fully protected by copyright. All requests for professional performance must be addressed to the author's agents, Casarotto Ramsay Ltd, National House, 60-66 Wardour Street, London W1V 3HP.

Rights of performance by amateurs are controlled by Samuel French Ltd, 52 Fitzroy Street, London W1P 6JR, and they, or their authorised agents, issue licences to amateurs on payment of a fee. **It is an infringement of the Copyright to give any performance or public reading of the play before the fee has been paid and the licence issued.**

The Royalty Fee is subject to contract and subject to variation at the sole discretion of Samuel French Ltd.

**When the Barbarians Came** was first professionally presented by Very Fine Productions at the New End Theatre, Hampstead on October 20th 1994, with the following cast:

| | |
|---|---|
| MARCUS | Sam Dastor |
| JULIA | Nina Marc |
| CAPTAIN ANTONY | Peter Czajkowski |
| ADRIAN | Don Taylor |
| AUGUSTUS | Neil Macleod |
| CLAUDIA | Sheila Mitchell |
| TARQUIN | Rick Warden |
| OCTAVIUS | Chris Chambers |
| LAVINIA | Lucy Taylor |
| CLOTEN | Rick Warden |
| ACTOR | Chris Chambers |
| SECRETARY | Lucy Taylor |

Designed by Martina Hildebrandt

Lighting by Tanya Burns

Produced by Adam Burr

Directed by Jon Harris

# WHEN THE BARBARIANS CAME

## By Don Taylor

## ACT ONE

*Large hollow drums beating, blaring low trumpets, like an Ancient Roman Triumph. Marching feet, a very large crowd, cheering wildly at a distance. A field gun salute. Jet planes fly past. Marcus enters. He is about forty, casually but expensively dressed. We see him in a pool of light, as he speaks to the audience.*

MARCUS: Everyone remembers what they were doing when the Barbarians came. As a matter of fact, I was in bed with Julia at the time. Afterwards, she got up, went into the other room, and turned on the television set. 'Marcus,' I heard her say, quietly, without any sense of panic. 'They're here.'

*The lights come up on Julia, standing looking at the TV set. She is naked but for a silk wrap. Bright sunlight pours in through an open window. There are clothes on the floor.*

I got up and went to the bedroom door, and saw her standing in her silk dressing gown in front of the screen, watching the procession entering the Imperial Gate. It was a hot afternoon and the windows were open. We could hear the sound of the cheering coming across the Park. We both stood there by the window, watching the pictures on the screen, with the sound turned down, listening to the cheering from the other side of the Park.

JULIA: Squadrons of cavalry, and enough infantry to populate a province. Drums and flags and screaming trumpets. They say it'll take more than two hours. Whatever we pretend to call it, it's a Victory Parade. Isn't it?

MARCUS: I suppose it's typical.

JULIA: What is ?

MARCUS: That I should be in bed. While history is being made.

JULIA: Typical of you maybe. Not me....

> *She begins to move about the room getting dressed. Marcus stays still.*

MARCUS: You were there too, I believe.

JULIA: And very pleasant it was.... But if anything really important had been going on....

MARCUS: I would have come a bad second.

JULIA: You would have been postponed to a more luxurious time. I'm not a ten minute job. I like to relax and enjoy myself.

MARCUS: Isn't it important then? The collapse of everything we've stood for for a thousand years?

JULIA: Oh yes, *that's* important. But that happened last week. This is just the Lord Mayor's Show.

MARCUS: This, my dear Julia, is an army of Goths entering unopposed through the Imperial Gate, and being welcomed by thousands of cheering people as the saviours of the city! Last time they came through that gate it was with a battering ram!

JULIA: But that's all history, my darling. This time we invited them in, by mass acclamation. If you're one of the acclaimers, you turn out and cheer. If not, you might just as well relax in bed and enjoy yourself. There's no one out there who matters, only plebs and P R men.

MARCUS: And an army of Goths.

JULIA: Rank and file darling, do what they're told, whoever's side they're on.

MARCUS: Like me.

JULIA: I can think of many things I might call you, Marcus, but rank and file's not one of them.

MARCUS: I won't ask you what.

JULIA: Thank you. ( *kissing him* ) That was very nice. We must do it again sometime.

MARCUS: You're in a hurry, all at once. Where are you going?

JULIA: I'll see you in about an hour. In the bar of The Palatine Hotel. Don't be late.

MARCUS: Why on earth are you going there?

JULIA: I have some people to meet.

*Julia sweeps offstage. The lights close round Marcus.*

MARCUS: I don't go to The Palatine Hotel. Nobody I know does, except Adrian - and that's because it's almost as over the top as he is, and he can usually find someone who'll buy him a drink. It's got an atrium, an outside glass lift that makes you sick, and a bar fifty yards long. But when Julia gives an order, people jump to it. Or at least, I do.

*Marcus goes offstage as the lights come up on a luxurious, rather vulgarly up-market bar in The Palatine Hotel. Julia is drinking with Adrian, to the sound of musak. Adrian is in his fifties, a voice mellowed by thirty years of continuous talk, washed down by enough gin to pickle most people for life.*

ADRIAN: I haven't a clue how I shall survive.

JULIA: Of course you'll survive, Adrian. You've survived for thirty years.

ADRIAN: Julia darling, these people are Barbarians, you do understand that don't you? They don't care about theatre.

JULIA: But you do, Adrian, you care passionately. So you'll make up for their lack.

ADRIAN: It's all very well to make jokes about it, but the situation's desperate. I have serious doubts as to whether the theatre will survive at all.

JULIA: Not to mention civilisation as we know it.

ADRIAN: The theatre is civilisation as we know it. I'll have another one of those, just to cheer me up.

JULIA: Mario, same again please.....

*The barman pours another large gin for Adrian.*

ADRIAN: Have you met any of them yet?

JULIA: Hardly. They've only just arrived.

ADRIAN: Their delegation's been here the best part of a month though. Extraordinary people. They all look exactly the same, with their tightly-buttoned suits, and their hair larded down with grease.

JULIA: That's just the top men, the military and the administration.

ADRIAN: And the way all their faces sort of shine, have you noticed? The men at least. Do you think they rub in a special gel to make their cheeks and foreheads glow like that?

JULIA: With Barbarians, anything is possible. Anyway, the rank and file aren't like that. Just plain Barbarians.

ADRIAN: Like we all see in our nightmares... Will there be rape and looting and burning down temples, like last time?

JULIA: No, of course not. Fire and the sword are very out of date.

ADRIAN: Or mass arrests at dawn? People who disappear?

JULIA: Now that is much more modern-sounding... I don't know. It's possible.

ADRIAN: I've been summoned to meet them at the Council of the Arts tomorrow. I'm scared stiff.

JULIA: And I'm called to a press briefing this evening. The new Minister of Information will be there himself, apparently.

ADRIAN: Oh, they won't touch journalists, that's for sure, and you political scribblers are the safest of the lot. How else can they spread their Barbarism but through the press? But artists are a dispensable luxury, we all know that.

JULIA: Just wait and see. Go along. Be your usual charming self. And don't get drunk.

ADRIAN: Easier said than done, when your whole livelihood is at stake.

JULIA: Not to mention your life!

ADRIAN: That will do Julia! You're a nasty little bitch, like all lady journalists. Thank God you never wrote theatre reviews.

*Captain Antony enters at the other end of the bar, and buys a drink. He is about thirty, very intelligent and self-possessed, the best type of career junior officer, with a neat short haircut, a well-cut casual suit, and an establishment tie. Julia notes his entry at once, without changing the tone of her speech at all.*

JULIA: It might come to that yet, now the Barbarians are here. Excuse me a moment, there's someone just come in I want to see.

ADRIAN: Anyone I know?

JULIA: No, Adrian, nobody you know.

*The lights crossfade to the other end of the bar as Julia moves across to meet Captain Antony.*

JULIA: Well, Captain, you're exactly on time. As a good military man should always be.

CAPTAIN ANTONY: Whereas journalists are nearly always early, I find, particularly if you meet them in a bar.

JULIA: I've been talking to poor Adrian. Do you know him?

CAPTAIN ANTONY: No, I don't think so.

JULIA: Runs the third largest theatre in the city, has done for years. On a massive and yearly increasing subsidy.

CAPTAIN ANTONY: Well. His days are numbered then.

JULIA: Indeed.

CAPTAIN ANTONY: Is he aware of that?

JULIA: I think he has an inkling. But he's a great fighter. Survived on the edge of bankruptcy since we were both in our cots... Well? What have you got for me?

CAPTAIN ANTONY: They're moving very fast. Their Leader's already installed in the Old Palace - she arrived in secret yesterday - and they're moving in, at every level of government and administration, with frightening speed and efficiency. All that marching and drumming is just for show. Every department, every quango, every committee already has its new men in place, or will have within two days.

JULIA: The police?

CAPTAIN ANTONY: The very first. And the Army. The whole High Command has been effectively demoted or retired. The Colonel of my own Regiment has gone, and his Major. As far as I can see all ranks of Colonel and above have been automatically replaced.

JULIA: What about you?

CAPTAIN ANTONY: It seems that junior officers are safe for the moment. But for how long, I don't know.

JULIA: Is it an invasion, or a revolution?

CAPTAIN ANTONY: It's both. We wanted them to save our bacon, but they've made it very plain it will be on their terms, not ours.

JULIA: So what about us? And people who think like us?

CAPTAIN ANTONY: Well, we're in a minority, as rational people always are. What these people are selling is simplicity. All those problems of yours that have seemed so intractable for a generation, we'll solve them for you. Like Alexander with his sword.

JULIA: One sharp cut.

CAPTAIN ANTONY: A good many more than one I should think.

JULIA: This is all off the record I suppose?

CAPTAIN ANTONY: More than that, it's dangerous. So keep it entirely to yourself. When we want the press, we'll tell you.

JULIA: What a shame! A terrific story, and I have to keep my mouth shut.

CAPTAIN ANTONY: Or they might shut it for you.

JULIA: Yes indeed.... So what do we do?

CAPTAIN ANTONY: For the moment, keep quiet and watch what happens. This is the honeymoon period, they've got massive popular support.

JULIA: It hardly seems possible! Only two years ago, I remember spending a whole afternoon sitting in a flat with a group of intellectual friends, discussing the real possibility of revolution! But not from this quarter!

CAPTAIN ANTONY: None of us took them seriously enough. There have always been Barbarians, but we thought we'd beaten them for good, centuries ago. We didn't recognise them in their modern dress.

JULIA: The question is, have they really changed? Or do they just wear different clothes?

CAPTAIN ANTONY: I suspect we shall know the answer to that very soon.

JULIA: And the meeting? Is it going ahead?

CAPTAIN ANTONY: Yes. Wednesday evening in Augustus' house, on the Collatine Hill.

JULIA: Oh, very swish! No plotting in dirty little attics with a single light bulb these days. Double drawing rooms, Victorian furniture, and stripped pine in the kitchen.

CAPTAIN ANTONY: The people there will all be of some weight. We're not playing revolutionary fantasy games you know. If you think we are, stay away.

JULIA: No, neither am I. Can I bring Marcus?

CAPTAIN ANTONY: Is he any use? Will he ever do anything?

JULIA: Well, he's pretty good in bed. But maybe he doesn't quite have what you call weight.

CAPTAIN ANTONY: Can he be trusted?

JULIA: I trust him.

CAPTAIN ANTONY: Not the same thing.

JULIA: And he does have money, not to mention a safe house in the country, and half a dozen flats here too.

CAPTAIN ANTONY: You might as well. I doubt if we will be able to keep our activities secret, even if we want to. The Barbarians are everywhere, and no doubt the security system was the first to be in place: so they'll soon find out what's what.... Excuse me, I must go.

*He finishes his drink.*

JULIA: I'll see you Wednesday

*Captain Antony goes.*

JULIA: ( *Finishing hers* ) God willing.

*She returns to where Adrian is sitting.*

ADRIAN: Really, Julia, you do talk to some extraordinarily disreputable people. I'd never trust you with any of my secrets.

JULIA: Do you have secrets, Adrian? Surely not?

ADRIAN: A few, angel heart, a few.

JULIA: Shall I buy you another?

ADRIAN: You can buy me several. The older I get the less it affects me.

JULIA: What? Theatrical disaster? Other people's opinions? Sex?

ADRIAN: Gin.

*The lights fade on the bar, and Marcus enters into a pool of light.*

MARCUS: When I got there twenty minutes later, Julia was sitting with Adrian, who was already pretty drunk, and the Captain - whose name was Antony, and whom I had not, at that stage, met - was gone. So I didn't meet him till the evening at Augustus' house, three days later....

*The lights come up on Augustus' house, and we hear a burst of conversation from about thirty voices, of both sexes, as Captain Antony comes up to Marcus.*

CAPTAIN ANTONY: Yes... Marcus, of course. I'm very glad to meet you.

MARCUS: The mysterious Captain Antony. Whenever I don't know what Julia's up to, she's usually with you.

CAPTAIN ANTONY: I don't think of myself as mysterious.

MARCUS: I suppose you're in Intelligence, are you?

CAPTAIN ANTONY: I'm a serving officer. And you, of course, I've heard of.

MARCUS: I can't think where.

CAPTAIN ANTONY: Well, from Julia, and....

MARCUS: I trained as a lawyer, but I hardly ever practise. One of the disadvantages of being born with money. One lacks the compulsion to work. What do you think of this crowd?

CAPTAIN ANTONY: Impressive.

MARCUS: The great and good of the city, all in one room. Who's that Julia's talking to?

CAPTAIN ANTONY: Octavius and Lavinia. Student leaders I think. I suppose I should say 'representatives'. I don't know them.

MARCUS: Neither do I. But I don't know anyone that matters. Except you now.

CAPTAIN ANTONY: Do I matter?

MARCUS: I assumed everyone mattered here except me.

CAPTAIN ANTONY: Well. You must matter too, or you wouldn't be here...

> *Captain Antony moves to one side of the stage for a drink as the lights emphasise Marcus. Marcus speaks to the audience, while the babble of conversation in the room continues at a low level.*

MARCUS: The Collatine Hill is one of the most sought-after areas of the city, wide curving avenues, plenty of trees, and beautiful old houses standing in huge leafy gardens, and Augustus' house, presided over by his remarkable wife, Claudia, is one of the most impressive. I recognised two playwrights, consciously avoiding each other, a well-known philosopher, and a successful novelist holding court by the drinks table. There were several journalists, of course, and three or four politicians, no longer with any real hope of power, principal among them Augustus himself, nearly seventy now, silver-haired, a veteran of three coalition Governments in the last twenty years, and with directorships in half a dozen top companies. When we all got ourselves seated, Augustus spoke for the best part of an hour...

> *Augustus enters as Marcus mentions him, while Marcus himself goes to the opposite side of the stage from Captain Antony. Augustus addresses the audience as though they were the people in his room. The various voices that call out during the scene are either planted in the audience, or recorded on speakers from the back, as are the crowd reaction noises, as required.*

AUGUSTUS: When the historians look back on us from the future... and I think they will look back, with interest, not contempt... they will see the progress of the most heroic struggle to reconcile what some might consider exclusive opposites. The need to progress in industry, and technology, the necessity to create wealth, so as to finance that progress, and at the same time, the need to look after our people, to give them a chance to live full, rich and productive lives....

*'Hear Hear,' and other noises of approval.*

AUGUSTUS: The reconciliation of these two great opposites has been the task we have set ourselves for three generations. And the fact is.... we all know this, or we wouldn't be sitting here tonight.... we have failed in that great task. The Barbarians are here. We invited them to come.

*Noise, some disagreement, 'No, No... I didn't invite them to come.... Hear hear!' etc.*

AUGUSTUS: And the first thing we must try to understand is why. What happened?

*An angry voice from the far end of the room.*

VOICE: We got it wrong, that's what happened.... you got it wrong, I should say, you politicians!

AUGUSTUS: I freely admit we got it wrong....

VOICE: Plenty of people were telling you at the time. In my second play, twenty years ago...

*Cries of protest, 'Oh shut up, sit down, what have plays got to do with it?' etc. drown Augustus and his heckler. Another voice is heard.*

SECOND VOICE: There's no point in arguing about who got it right and who got it wrong. You ask why the Barbarians are here, and I'll tell you. Because there was so little sense of vision from any of our leaders that we spent all our time in petty sectional struggles, so that none of us noticed how pissed off with the whole process the mass of the plebs was becoming! If we were all out for our own ends, so could they be, and they'd support anyone at all who seemed to offer a future for them....!

*Noise, argument.*

AUGUSTUS: I speak as a member of three Governments, and I must admit to my share of the blame....

*A burst of conversation and argument.*

AUGUSTUS: But we were trying to do a very complicated thing, to reconcile the need for freedom with the need for justice, the need for equality. No one any longer believes that justice and equality can be imposed on a people by tyranny. That might be necessary when a nation is emerging from a state of feudalism into the modern world, but as soon as it achieves any success, it destroys the only justification for its existence. That belief was the platform we built on...

VOICE: And your house collapsed in ruins!

AUGUSTUS: But true democracy, of the spirit as well as the belly, is the most difficult game yet devised by the human race, it may take us generations to learn how to play it...

VOICE: You won't have time, the Barbarians have come, and they will bring all those kinds of games to an end!

*Confused noise and argument. Augustus shakes his head and moves across to talk with Antony. The lights focus on Marcus, and the argument fades under his voice as he speaks.*

MARCUS: At that point the meeting degenerated into a shouting match between the hard left, and the libertarian right, as these kinds of meetings so often do. All-embracing ideologies were laid out like grid systems, leaving no room for argument, only angry assertion. That might have been the end of it. But the situation now is so serious that people got fed up with both sets of ideologues, and asked them to leave, which they did, with a great deal of angry shouting about the dustbin of history and the sterility of intellectuals.... Those of us who remained tried to get back to some kind of sanity.

*Augustus comes back to centre stage, tired, defeated, but determined to be heard.*

AUGUSTUS: I asked Captain Antony to prepare a report for us on the situation as he now sees it, and how it is likely to develop....

*Sporadic clapping, murmured conversation, as Antony prepares to speak.*

CAPTAIN ANTONY: The military unit in which I serve... has made it its business to find out what has actually been done, and what is going to be done in the immediate future by our new masters... They intend, within the week, to stop the issue of free corn to the plebs completely...

*Disbelief, whistles of amazement, muttered cries of 'They can't do that...there'll be riots in the streets!' etc.....*

CAPTAIN ANTONY: ... to close down all the shipyards on the river and the estuary... the Greeks build ships better and cheaper, they think...

*Disbelief, anger.*

CAPTAIN ANTONY: ... to scrap all public works, workers' tenement housing and the like, and to reduce all expenditure on public programmes to nil, as soon as possible.

*As each new point is made the reaction is less extreme, more stunned.*

CAPTAIN ANTONY: Within a few weeks, they will present a whole new programme of laws to the senate, concerning the rights of the plebs to form workers' associations, and the legal standing of the Tribunes of the People, which will severely limit their possibilities of action, if they don't make them politically negligible.....

*Angry murmurs of disbelief, near panic. Octavius, a young man of twenty, comes up on stage, followed by Lavinia, of a similar age.*

OCTAVIUS: Can we speak, on behalf of the Students' Action Committee?

AUGUSTUS: Please do....

OCTAVIUS: We aren't taken in by the appearance of legality, bills to do this and that...

LAVINIA: We think it is only a matter of time before they begin a policy of mass arrests and deportations of all activists.

OCTAVIUS: We have voted the immediate formation of student militias, to link up with workers' militias, and be ready to fight for our liberty.

LAVINIA: We urge you not to be deceived by smooth talk and apparent sophistication. These people are Barbarians, however they present themselves these days. And Barbarians have only one underlying purpose in their hearts - to destroy!

*The students provoke some applause and cheering, and Julia goes across to engage them in conversation. After a few moments she walks out with them, still talking, as though to the terrace.*

MARCUS: There was a lot more in the same vein, and it impressed people who have a taste for that kind of thing. Julia was particularly taken with Octavius and Lavinia, and talked to them for the best part of an hour, in the drawing room, and out on the terrace.

*After a moment Julia returns. As the lights focus on Marcus and Augustus, Julia and Antony come together, talking and pouring drinks, in a late evening/early morning shaded light, as though all the others have gone and they are left alone talking.*

MARCUS: The meeting went on till after midnight, with everyone getting more and more intense, as we all began to realise the full horror of what had happened to our city. By two o'clock there was only a hard core of us left.....

*Marcus crosses to join the others.*

AUGUSTUS: Do you think those kids are right? That the only answer will be blood in the streets?

CAPTAIN ANTONY: Students always think it will be blood in the streets. When it is, it's usually their own.

AUGUSTUS: I keep on re-running things in my mind. Decisions. Would it have been different if this or that had gone another way?

CLAUDIA: You made the best judgement you could at the time. No honest man can do otherwise.

AUGUSTUS: There were too many things I knew to be wrong. Too many compromises.

JULIA: It's an old man's vice, Augustus. Not your business. Leave it to the historians.

AUGUSTUS: That's what terrifies me.

CLAUDIA: What do historians know about anything? You have to be alive at the time, to know what it felt like.

MARCUS: What should we do?

JULIA: There's a question, from you, my darling! You will do what you always do. Nothing. Marcus is the perpetual observer. Every nation needs one.

MARCUS: I should like to know. For when they come knocking on my door.

AUGUSTUS: They won't come knocking on your door. They might on mine. What do you think, Antony? Is a purge in their line?

CAPTAIN ANTONY: In the past they would have slaughtered everyone, burned down the palaces, and set up their sheds in the ruins. But they're much more sophisticated these days.

JULIA: They don't burn down palaces any more. They live in them.

MARCUS: You still haven't answered my question. I'm a simple soul. Do I hide, or pretend nothing has happened, or run screaming into the streets?

JULIA: Or oil your Kalashnikov, like Octavius and Lavinia?

CAPTAIN ANTONY: It's impossible to say. All we get from them at the moment is orders, but that will have to change. They can't rule us like a conquered population. We shall just have to wait, and keep our eyes and ears open...

*Augustus gestures to Antony and they go off talking together. Julia and Marcus speak quietly.*

MARCUS: Are you coming back with me tonight?

JULIA: Oh no, darling, really, I'm shattered! Far too tired!

MARCUS: You can sleep with me as well as anyone else.

JULIA: But not as well as by myself. I'll call in tomorrow for coffee. Take care...

MARCUS: I'll walk you home.

JULIA: You don't need to. Not now the Barbarians are here... ( *With an ironical grin* ) The streets haven't been so safe for an unaccompanied woman for years.

*She goes offstage, leaving Marcus in his pool of light.*

MARCUS: So I left her there, and walked home alone, in a night warm as velvet, and under a quite unbelievably beautiful moon. I kept on asking myself, how could it have happened? I knew all the answers, but they didn't convince...... A week later, Adrian invited me to have lunch with him at his theatre.....

*Marcus walks across to Adrian in the restaurant/bar of Adrian's theatre, where we hear the sound of fifteen or twenty occupied lunch tables. As Marcus sits, Adrian is in mid-flow.*

ADRIAN: Of course, I was terrified, and very depressed. I thought, well, thirty years of struggle comes to an end here! I couldn't imagine why else they wanted to see me. So, I was there on the dot, and went in like a schoolboy summoned to see the Head.

MARCUS: And you met one? A real Barbarian?

ADRIAN: Yes, but, what a surprise! To start with, of course, it was in the old Council of the Arts Director's Office - I've sat on that chair a few times in the last twenty years, I can tell you - I mean, it is a rather grand and elegant classical building, beautifully furnished - but you could hardly say he looked out of place.

MARCUS: And what happened? Self-evidently you weren't fired.

ADRIAN: Well, he came to the door and shook hands with me, with a very pleasant sort of smile... he was very happy to meet me, and he'd admired my work for years... and that was a bit of a surprise too, I didn't think these people knew me from Adam. He has large round glasses, slicked-back black greased hair, like they all do, and of course, the regulation suit and tie. They all seem to dress very respectably, but forty years out of date, if you know what I mean...

MARCUS: Not quite savages then...?

ADRIAN: Not at all, they don't wear shaggy skins any more or have stinking lard smeared all over their bodies. They're not medieval devils either, with horns and bad breath and their hind quarters matted with shit - like some people we know! Very patrician in manner they are these days, like the eldest sons of some of our more old-fashioned families. A bit passé, a bit out of date.

MARCUS: So what happened?

ADRIAN: We talked for an hour or so, and then, my dear, the biggest surprise of the lot! A white-jacketed waiter wheeled in an elegant little lunch, open sandwiches, prawns, lobster, the lot, and a delightful bottle of white Burgundy! And I thought to myself, well, if this is Barbarism, it's not so bad!

MARCUS: I mean about the theatre?

ADRIAN: Well, I went in there expecting nothing. And I came out with something. I survived, so I suppose in our business that counts as a triumph.

MARCUS: And why have you invited me to have lunch with you... apart from the pleasure of your company, which is, as always, considerable...?

ADRIAN: Ah, Marcus, what a dear chap you are!... Now... well... to begin with, the subsidy is still in place.

MARCUS: Really!

ADRIAN: Frozen at its present level for one year. But, of course, with thirty per cent inflation, that's not quite as good as it sounds.

MARCUS: A cut of about a third, in fact.

ADRIAN: Indeed. But my dear, I was expecting nothing! So to come out with two thirds intact was more than my wildest dreams...

MARCUS: But how are you going to manage? You've been walking a financial tightrope for years ...

ADRIAN: Of course I have, it's nothing new. I must make some economies, of course, and I must do, for this year at least, a rather more popular programme than I had originally planned, but...

MARCUS: You still won't make ends meet, surely?

ADRIAN: No. And that's where you come in.

MARCUS: Me?

ADRIAN: Marcus, dear boy, you have money...

MARCUS: Oh, but really, none to invest in the theatre...

ADRIAN: Of course not, I'm not asking for that, nobody in his right mind ever puts his own money in the theatre. It's quite the opposite, I intend to pay you money, not you give it to me.

MARCUS: What do you mean?

ADRIAN: You have always lived with money, you were brought up with it, you have the feel of it in your bones...!

MARCUS: Well, Adrian...

ADRIAN: I want you to join me here, as my principal fund-raiser.

MARCUS: Me?

ADRIAN: You. I'm offering you a job, Marcus.

MARCUS: A job. I haven't had a job in years.

ADRIAN: Well, you have one now... if you want it.

MARCUS: What would I have to do?

ADRIAN: Make up that one third cut in funding, and if possible, exceed it: by going to business, commerce, property, advertising, whoever you like, and persuading them that the one thing they want to do is to sponsor my theatre.

MARCUS: Good God!

ADRIAN: That's the only way it's going to be possible now, Marcus. It's that, or the theatre will die. They won't pay for it any more. I don't expect my grant to increase in the future, on the contrary, it'll get steadily smaller. This isn't a change of heart, just a delayed execution. They're looking for the time when I don't need anything from them at all, and pretty soon too. That's where you come in. Without someone like you, I can't possibly survive, no theatre will! Thinking about whom I could trust, and would have the contacts to do it, it was obvious: it had to be you.

MARCUS: I'm very flattered... but I've never done anything like it before....

ADRIAN: None of us has. But by golly, we'll learn, and fast! They've thrown all the old Arts people out, double quick, all those academics and critics who believed the Arts belong to all the people, all that crowd, are in the dustbin. In their place they've brought in a whole lot of administration and management types, our own people, not Barbarians. Do you remember that appalling twerp, Claudius? Was General Administrator of two or three small provincial theatres in the last ten years or so, made a terrible hash of all of them? He's now financial director for a whole group of theatres, including mine.

MARCUS: The man's an utter mediocrity. Completely second-rate.

ADRIAN: Of course he is! That's the point. They're staffing the whole arts-funding business with mediocrities. The one thing people like that love is real power. You should see old Claude parading around there, wearing his Barbarian suit and tie, and smirking fit to bust his face! They love nothing better than being able to order first-rate people about, and if they can make them go down on their knees and beg, so much the better! They're ideal people to put the Barbarians' policies into action.

MARCUS: Well, you're still first-rate, Adrian, whatever else you are!

ADRIAN: Oh, dear boy, you are so kind! A bit tattered after thirty years I think, a bit shot to pieces, but the old battle-flag is still just about flying. Well? Will you join me? I promise you, it will be exciting.

MARCUS: Well.... I'll think about it.

> *We hear a slight scuffle, as though someone is arguing with the head waiter, and a young actor approaches the table..*

ACTOR: Look... Adrian... I'm sorry to interrupt you at lunch... (*To Marcus*) please excuse me, sir.... but I've been trying to get an appointment with you for over a week, and I must talk to you about my contract. Can you possibly fit me in this afternoon, please? I'm very sorry to interrupt....

ADRIAN: Yes, yes, of course I can fit you in, dear boy. Look in at three... no, better make it half past....

ACTOR: Thank you, Adrian, thank you very much....

ADRIAN: Not at all, dear boy, we'll have a good natter...

ACTOR: Thanks.... Do excuse me...

> *The Actor goes away. The whole scene has been cringingly embarrassing, the actor moved by sheer desperation, Adrian very angry at being interrupted in what he considers the most important business, but hiding it behind a standard professional charm.*

ADRIAN: Sorry about that. Rather embarrassing.

MARCUS: Was it?

ADRIAN: What's said and what's unsaid, you know... I'm going to have to sack him this afternoon. He doesn't know that yet. He thinks we're haggling about his fee for the next two years.

MARCUS: That seems a shame.

ADRIAN: Oh yes, it is, he's a good young actor, very promising. But what can I do? I have to cut the company by at least a third next season. Seven or eight of them will have to go.

MARCUS: Tell me.... how can you offer to pay me money to work for you, when you are sacking a third of your actors?

ADRIAN: Oh well, that's simple dear boy. Actors cost money. You, I hope, are going to earn some. Shall we have another bottle of that? It's really rather good, isn't it.....

*Marcus rises from the table, and the light and the restaurant noise fades till Marcus is alone in his pool of light.*

MARCUS: I brooded on Adrian's offer for a week. I'd always known theatre people, and liked their company, but never thought of working with them. But the idea of that hand-to-mouth existence gradually began to attract me. Not that I needed the money. I could give it up at any time, as far as that was concerned. But it seemed that it might be amusing, to get to the heart of where the money comes from. And what else was there to do, now the Barbarians had come? Hardly law, which had bored me for years anyway. I made up my mind, phoned Adrian, and told him I accepted. 'I knew you would, dear boy,' he said, and when I asked him how, he laughed his smoke-dried laugh and said, 'just instinct,' whatever that's supposed to mean. Nothing, I suspect. The illusion of meaning, where in fact there is none. Like a lot of theatre.... So, after a gap of a good many years, I was actually doing again, instead of merely watching. I bought a bottle of champagne, and went round to Julia's to celebrate.

*Marcus moves across to an area which represents the hallway of Julia's flat.*

JULIA: Darling, congratulations, what a marvellous idea!

MARCUS: Well, it could be interesting.

JULIA: I've always wanted to know a really big wheel in the theatre.

MARCUS: I shall hardly be that. But it should be fun. You can help me to drink this bottle of champagne, and we'll spend the rest of the evening in bed, eh?....

JULIA: Shhh.... not now.

MARCUS: Why not now?

JULIA: No, be a good boy. I've got a visitor....

MARCUS: A visitor? Who?

JULIA: Captain Antony. He's in the next room. We've just had dinner.

MARCUS: Oh..... well....

JULIA: No, no, don't be silly, you don't have to go. Business, business, that's all. Come through.

MARCUS: Well... I don't know...

JULIA: I said come through....!

*They move across the stage to meet Captain Antony.*

JULIA: Antony, Marcus is here with the most thrilling news. He's going to work for Adrian at his theatre. Raising funds.

CAPTAIN ANTONY: Many congratulations....

MARCUS: Thank you.... thank you...

JULIA: And he's brought a bottle of... oh, very good champagne, to celebrate.

CAPTAIN ANTONY: A wise move, I should say, in the circumstances.

MARCUS: Oh, really?

CAPTAIN ANTONY: Quite certainly.... Have you met any of them yet?

MARCUS: Who?

CAPTAIN ANTONY: The Barbarians.

MARCUS: No, not yet. Though now I shall, I imagine.

JULIA: You'll get a surprise. Won't he? I certainly did.

CAPTAIN ANTONY: Most people I know have done.

MARCUS: Well, yes. Adrian was telling me. Very civilised apparently. Very courteous, not to say flattering.

CAPTAIN ANTONY: And very, very clever. Not at all what anyone was expecting.

JULIA: Everyone was rushing indoors, turning all the locks and shooting the bolts, and waiting for the security police to come. And what happened? Nothing.

CAPTAIN ANTONY: Or the phone rang, and they got offered a job. Some of them did. Very clever.

MARCUS: Am I part of a trend then?

CAPTAIN ANTONY: I wouldn't say that. But have you heard of anyone at all being arrested, tortured, shot?

MARCUS: No.

CAPTAIN ANTONY: Or harmed in any way?

MARCUS: No. I don't think so.

CAPTAIN ANTONY: I don't know anyone who has.

JULIA: Everyone was expecting... I don't know what. Unimaginable horrors. Well, you were at that meeting. It just hasn't happened.

CAPTAIN ANTONY: What has happened is that a very large number of people have lost their jobs. Mainly plebs, factories closing, whole industries being shut down. But a good many equestrian class too, managers, teachers, administrators.

JULIA: And in particular, anyone who has expressed themselves in any way antipathetic to the Barbarians. So you'd better keep your mouth shut, darling.

MARCUS: Oh well. I'm not antipathetic to anyone.

CAPTAIN ANTONY: That seems to be their policy. No oppression. Just the sack.

*Julia opens the champagne.*

JULIA: There.... Cheers!

CAPTAIN ANTONY: Cheers, and congratulations!

MARCUS: Cheers!... thank you.

JULIA: And good luck hunting out all the money!

*They drink.*

MARCUS: Has no one at all been arrested? It's hard to believe.

CAPTAIN ANTONY: It may just be a phoney war. But I don't think so. They've taken us by surprise, like any good political tactician should.

MARCUS: And what about all those people out of work?

CAPTAIN ANTONY: The vast majority of them are poor, and have no power, particularly now the Tribunes of the People have been emasculated. But that's the one unpredictable question. How much will people take before they say, 'OK we've had enough'?

MARCUS: What about Tamora? Presumably it all comes from the top?

CAPTAIN ANTONY: Very few people ever see her. They've shut her away in the Old Palace like a Queen Bee, and she may very well have gone mad by now.

JULIA: But they're still scared to death of her. She was the traditional Barbarian Queen, twice as cruel as any man, to make up for her sex. They know one word from her and they've had it.

CAPTAIN ANTONY: But she's not actually in charge now.

MARCUS: Who is?

JULIA: Nobody knows.

CAPTAIN ANTONY: I met a chap two days ago who was actually one of her advisors, a non-Barbarian, fellow named Timothy.

MARCUS: Good God. Advisor to the Goths. What an honour!

CAPTAIN ANTONY: Well, he's that sort of man. You don't have to be very cynical to know that there are a good many people in the world who will do absolutely anything for money, and even more for power. He says that when you look into her eyes, you see a kind of cavernous sincerity, empty, but terrifying. It's a simple philosophy all right, Barbarism. But they mean it.

MARCUS: What a fearful prospect.

CAPTAIN ANTONY: Well. Maybe not quite as fearful as we have imagined. For a good many people at least. Are you terrified? Or have you got a job?

MARCUS: Well. I suppose I've got a job.

CAPTAIN ANTONY: And who are you working for? Ultimately?

MARCUS: Yes..... I see what you mean.

CAPTAIN ANTONY: Excuse me, Julia. Thank you so much for dinner, and the discussion. I enjoyed both, but... I really think I ought to go now....

MARCUS: Oh, please don't go on my account...

CAPTAIN ANTONY: No, it's not mere politeness. I do have an appointment later this evening. And I think we'd more or less finished, hadn't we?

JULIA: Yes, I think so....

CAPTAIN ANTONY: So, if you'll excuse me. Thanks for the champagne. It was very good.

*Julia takes Captain Antony to the door, and then returns to Marcus. There is a pause.*

JULIA: It's very childish of you to sulk.

MARCUS: I'm not sulking.

JULIA: You don't think so?

MARCUS: I really don't see...

JULIA: I'm sorry I wasn't alone to share your celebration in quite the way you planned. You didn't tell me anything about it. You just dropped in here, quite uninvited.

MARCUS: Oh, well, if that's the situation....

JULIA: No it isn't, sit down, and stop being a fool. There's half a bottle of champagne left. Let's drink it.

*She pours two glasses of champagne.*

MARCUS: Julia..... what's going on?

JULIA: What do you mean, what's going on?

MARCUS: With you and Antony.

JULIA: Nothing.

MARCUS: I don't believe you.

JULIA: I'm not your property, Marcus. We're very good friends, we've been lovers for just over a year, but you don't have any rights over me, or who I meet, or who I go to bed with, come to that.

MARCUS: No. But I do have a certain amount of fastidiousness about whom I go to bed with.

JULIA: Anyway, you're jumping to conclusions. There's no question of that... Listen. There's been nobody except you, since we began. Really.

MARCUS: So I repeat, what's going on? I'm not a fool. Whenever I turn my back, you're with Antony, or meeting him, or planning to met him.

JULIA: All right.... now look, Marcus.... just keep this to yourself, will you?

MARCUS: Keep what to myself?

JULIA: Something is going on. With Antony. He's up to something.

MARCUS: Up to what?

JULIA: I don't know, but it's to do with the coming of the Barbarians. I don't know what yet. But I intend to find out. You understand?

MARCUS: Yes. I understand.

JULIA: Now. Let's drink that champagne, and then go to bed. And forget we ever had this conversation...

> *The lights fade on Marcus and Julia, and after a few seconds Marcus re-appears in the pool of light..*

MARCUS: Two weeks later, I arranged a meeting with Augustus. I'd already had the promise of some money, from the obvious sources, but nothing like enough. It seemed to me that Augustus was as likely as anyone to know where the real money is, the blood that keeps the whole body moving. What I didn't know was that, as I was going to Augustus' house on the Collatine Hill, Antony had arranged a very private meeting in an obscure square in the suburbs - and that Julia wasn't far behind him......

> *Marcus crosses the stage. The lights change, with goboes to suggest a square full of trees.*

MARCUS: The square is quite big, and full of umbrella pines, well-spaced, with beautiful soft-needled walks, a quiet café, that is never too crowded, at the centre, and plenty of benches to enjoy the view and the almost intoxicating scent of the trees. It's a favourite place for lovers, or for friends to talk seriously. So Captain Antony, not in uniform, talking to Octavius and Lavinia in their student jeans and T shirts, didn't look out of place.

> *Marcus exits as the lights come up on Captain Antony talking to Octavius and Lavinia, all three seated on a bench, or on chairs round a cafe table. They talk quietly, not conspiratorially, but aware of the danger of being*

*overheard. Octavius and Lavinia are troubled, Captain Antony as calm and detached as ever.*

CAPTAIN ANTONY: Of course, I have been on the campus three or four times in the last month, and at some impassioned meetings too...

LAVINIA: You've been up into University City?

CAPTAIN ANTONY: I pass perfectly easily for a graduate student, or one of the younger dons.

*A bleak pause.*

OCTAVIUS: Spying on us.

CAPTAIN ANTONY: Not at all. If you are thinking of marrying someone, you do try to find out a little about the family, and what kind of dowry might be on offer. If you call that spying....

LAVINIA: How many other soldiers and policemen are up there on the campus, pretending to be graduate students or young dons?

CAPTAIN ANTONY: Some, you may be sure, unless the security branch is falling down on its job. Come on, you can hardly be surprised at that. It isn't only since the Barbarians came that that sort of thing has been going on.

OCTAVIUS: No, of course not, but....

CAPTAIN ANTONY: You know perfectly well who I am and what I'm doing. I need to use my eyes. See what you do, as well as what you say.

LAVINIA: And what have you seen?

CAPTAIN ANTONY: A great deal of anger and passion, a great deal of idealism. Exactly what I would expect from the intelligent young.

LAVINIA: Don't be cynical about it. It's real. There's no pretending.

OCTAVIUS: And it's eighty to ninety per cent. The ones who don't join us on the demonstrations and at the meetings aren't against us - just timid.

CAPTAIN ANTONY: Yes. We're all timid, human beings. Even the heroes. We know how fragile we are. How easily we can be broken.

*An uneasy pause.*

OCTAVIUS: Do you think it will come to that?

*The pause is not resolved.*

CAPTAIN ANTONY: You spoke very passionately at Augustus' house, about forming militias, making pacts with workers. I've seen plenty of enthusiasm. But I haven't seen that.

LAVINIA: We sent a deputation into the car factory, and another to a meeting of the transport workers.

OCTAVIUS: And to the big chemical plant outside the city, and the sulphur mines too.

CAPTAIN ANTONY: And?

OCTAVIUS: Great enthusiasm. But we didn't succeed in making any plans.

CAPTAIN ANTONY: Because twenty per cent of them have already been sacked, and the rest are nervous for their jobs.

OCTAVIUS: I suppose so.

CAPTAIN ANTONY: Enthusiasm isn't enough. The point is, when the day comes, can you deliver? I've spoken to a lot of people, utterly dedicated to the overthrow of the Barbarians and the recreation of the Old Republic, and they are going to need a great deal more than enthusiasm before they make a move. There may be millions in the streets. But revolutions aren't made by unarmed millions, not if governments have guns and are prepared to use them. They are made by small and highly-trained units, who know where to strike, and when. The Army has some. But they will need armed support from the population, not just cheering.

OCTAVIUS: We will have... some too.

CAPTAIN ANTONY: Some may not be enough.

LAVINIA: There's been a whole new regime at the University in the last three weeks, decrees from the Central University Council. Nothing repressive, no arrests, no restriction of freedom of speech, we can hold meetings, march, shout slogans. But it isn't happening anymore, not half as much....

CAPTAIN ANTONY: I can guess why.

LAVINIA: They have imposed a much stricter work routine. Every month there is to be a full assessment and review of progress, attendance and discipline, as well as quality of work. We daren't miss a single lecture or seminar any more. We could be thrown out of the University.

OCTAVIUS: Which means that the majority won't dare to take their noses out of their books anymore.

LAVINIA: We still have meetings, but less and less well-attended. They have us well tied, like a goat on a rope.

CAPTAIN ANTONY: I see.

OCTAVIUS: Everybody's scared, losing the grant, being sent away, no job at the end of it.

LAVINIA: Nobody wants to end up like the plebs.

CAPTAIN ANTONY: So, what you're saying, is that all that at the meeting was just rhetoric.

LAVINIA: For a real crisis they'll come out. Anyone arrested, deported, shot. No one would think twice.

CAPTAIN ANTONY: But no one's going to be. And, if a few are, you won't ever hear about it.

LAVINIA: I suppose not.

OCTAVIUS: It's not as bad as we expected. It just isn't serious enough. People won't take the risk.

CAPTAIN ANTONY: It is serious enough. It gets more serious every day. All you're saying is that it doesn't affect you....

OCTAVIUS: We have to go. It's dangerous sitting here.

CAPTAIN ANTONY: Of course. I understand.

OCTAVIUS: We'll keep in touch.

CAPTAIN ANTONY: Yes. We must.

> *There seems nothing more to say. Octavius and Lavinia look at each other irresolutely. Then they go together, without saying any more.*
>
> *Antony watches them for a moment, then takes a notebook from his pocket and writes in it. Julia comes on stage, watching him at a distance.*
>
> *As he closes the notebook and rises, Julia walks across to him, as though meeting him by accident.*

JULIA: Captain Antony....! What a surprise to see you here!

CAPTAIN ANTONY: Hallo, Julia. I could say the same.

JULIA: Oh, this is a favourite spot of mine, this little square. I often drive down here at the end of an afternoon, for a cup of coffee or a drink at the bar, and a quiet stroll under the pine trees.

CAPTAIN ANTONY: It's a novelty for me. I had to visit a specialist bookshop two streets away over there, and I chanced on the place by accident. I don't get over this side of town very often.

JULIA: Did you get it?

CAPTAIN ANTONY: Get what?

JULIA: The book you wanted.

CAPTAIN ANTONY: Oh, no. I had to place an order.

JULIA: I thought perhaps you were meeting someone here. It's very popular for that purpose.

CAPTAIN ANTONY: No. I'm not in love at the moment.

JULIA: Can I give you a lift back into town?

CAPTAIN ANTONY: Oh, that's very kind of you. Yes, if it's not too inconvenient.

JULIA: My car's over on this side of the square...

CAPTAIN ANTONY: I saw you somewhere unexpected the other night too.

JULIA: Really? Where?

CAPTAIN ANTONY: Going into Andreas' Restaurant. Far too expensive for a poor serving officer.

JULIA: And for me.

CAPTAIN ANTONY: With three Barbarians.

JULIA: A very boring evening it was too. But then, that's the job sometimes. Press attachés. Feeding me the Barbarian version.

CAPTAIN ANTONY: Did it convince?

JULIA: Not in the least. But the cuisine did. Andreas hasn't lost his touch since the Barbarians came. If anything, he's refined it. Here's my car.

CAPTAIN ANTONY: Thank you....

> *The lights fade as they go off, and come up, almost at once, on another part of the stage, representing Augustus' house, to indicate simultaneous time.*
>
> *Augustus enters with Marcus, to Claudia. Both men are drinking good wine. Claudia is not drinking..*

AUGUSTUS: .... Well, Marcus, I'm delighted you came to see me, and we're both full of congratulation at your job, aren't we, Claudia?

> *Claudia is lofty and aristocratic, the dark-toned voice of a great beauty grown old.*

CLAUDIA: It must be satisfying to be doing something really worth while.

MARCUS: Oh, do you think so? A lot of people think the theatre rather frivolous.

CLAUDIA: Only foolish people.

MARCUS: And I've done nothing for so long, it feels strange to be so busy. I look at my diary and don't see a single free afternoon.

AUGUSTUS: Have you hunted out any money yet?

MARCUS: Some. I need to find a great deal more.

CLAUDIA: It shouldn't be necessary. In a civilised country.

AUGUSTUS: It shouldn't be necessary, my dear, but we are no longer a civilised country, and it is.

MARCUS: I have a list of about eight or ten companies and financial groups I intend to contact. But I wanted your advice first. I know a good many of the people of course.....

AUGUSTUS: I can guess who most of them are. Some will help you. They know the Barbarians are very keen on this sort of thing, in the short term at least. So they'll be prepared to play along with you for a while.

MARCUS: Yes, I see.

AUGUSTUS: These people are hard. Don't expect anything for nothing. They'll give you money if they think they can get something tangible for it, not otherwise.

MARCUS: I've already learned that.

AUGUSTUS: It's up to you to offer them a good deal.

MARCUS: I was hoping that you might...

AUGUSTUS: Me? I've no money for the theatre. I wouldn't give it to Adrian if I had.

MARCUS: It wasn't money I wanted.... Your name.

AUGUSTUS: My name? A discredited politician?

MARCUS: That's not how they see it. Or the business community.

We want you to be a kind of flagship for us. A patron, if you like.

AUGUSTUS: Tell him.

MARCUS: What?

CLAUDIA: We're leaving the city. Going to live on our estate in the South. For good. The rest of our lives.

AUGUSTUS: Which, in the nature of things, won't be very long.

MARCUS: But... the meeting we held here, everything that was said...?

AUGUSTUS: Well. We all enjoyed it, I'm sure.

MARCUS: I see.

AUGUSTUS: I've sold up all my major financial holdings, resigned all my directorships, and I'm getting out. So, if you've come here looking for the one big wheel that moves all the others, you've come to the wrong place.

MARCUS: Whom have you sold to?

AUGUSTUS: You'll be shocked if I tell you.

MARCUS: I doubt that. I've seen enough by now.

AUGUSTUS: I've sold up to the Barbarians..... You see, you are shocked.

MARCUS: Well....

AUGUSTUS: A consortium of Barbarian business men, who are snapping up whole areas of industry and commerce in the wake of the take-over. They offered by far the best price. All the prudent money is leaving the city in boatloads. They weren't born here, they're not educated like us, but their money's good.

MARCUS: I see.

CLAUDIA: You can drop the critical tone, Marcus.

AUGUSTUS: All right, Claudia...

MARCUS: It wasn't critical.

CLAUDIA: For nearly thirty years my husband has given his life's blood for this city. He's done everything he can to make it a place fit for civilised people to live in. And what's his reward after all that time? The people would rather have the Barbarians. Very well. Let them have them, and good luck to them. We're getting out of it, going to the South. We have enough money to live there in great comfort, and in peace.

AUGUSTUS: Nevertheless, I can give you a few names of some of the new men that might help you...

MARCUS: Thank you.

CLAUDIA: I was born a patrician, brought up in the city, and on one of the great estates only a day's ride away. We were taught to respect the Gods, serve the Republic, and care for our fellow men. We were the greatest Empire the world had ever seen, it seemed that the sun would never set on such splendour. There were poor people and rich people, of course, plebs and slaves as well as Senators and Consuls, but we were all one great national family. The rich knew their duty to the poor, and the poor accepted their place in the scheme of things. Great men were on earth when I was a child, men who did great things. I'm seventy-one now, and, in one lifetime, I've seen it all decay, and become corrupted, and destroyed. Till now these savages have come, people we didn't even bother to have contempt for when I was a child, and they've taken over everything, and it's quite plain they are going to destroy everything. We will become just another tribe of Barbarians, while the torch of civilisation is passed on to some other people. Why should we stay in the city to watch that? Or even care, one way or the other?

*She walks slowly out of the room.*

AUGUSTUS: Claudia is very bitter. It matters to her even more than she says.

MARCUS: I can see.

AUGUSTUS: It's a fantasy, of course. There have been Barbarians on the boards of public companies for years. Even in the great days of the Republic. But she doesn't remember that.

MARCUS: I feel sorry for her.

AUGUSTUS: You need not. We've both had a very good deal from life. Save your sympathy for the ones who haven't. And go and see this fellow, on this number. His name's Tarquin, he's small and sharp, like a little predator, he hardly ever smiles, and his eyes are like a pair of ice-picks. But he's the rising man among the younger corporate sponsors. He's not yet thirty, and if it's live money you want, he'll know where to get it.....

*The lights change, Augustus and Claudia go off, while Marcus comes downstage into a pool of light.*

MARCUS: I didn't get back from Augustus' house till after midnight. When I did, I found a message from Julia on the answerphone.

*He looks up, and we hear Julia's recorded voice on the answerphone.*

JULIA: ( *On Answerphone* ) ... Marcus, listen... ring me and come round as soon as you get in, whatever time it is. I have something very important to tell you. About our friend Captain Antony.

*The answerphone clicks off, and we hear the end tone.*

MARCUS: I didn't need telling twice. I got straight into the car and drove to Julia's flat just south of the Forum. I didn't get there till one-fifteen.....

*The lights come up on Julia's flat, early morning, and Marcus crosses towards Julia, who is already on stage.*

JULIA: .... He'd told me he was busy all today and couldn't see me... this was several days ago... so I decided I would just keep an eye on him, see what he was actually up to when I wasn't around. So I staked out his flat from first light, and followed him.

MARCUS: And?

JULIA: He spent the whole morning at the Ministry of Defence.

MARCUS: Well, that's reasonable. He's a soldier.

JULIA: Yes, but what kind of soldier? I've never seen or heard of him doing anything that I'd call soldiering.

MARCUS: Well, he's in Intelligence, that's obvious, he was before the Barbarians came. Works undercover half the time I daresay.

JULIA: I'm sure of it. Have you ever asked him what he does?

MARCUS: Waste of time. He's not going to say 'I'm a secret service agent,' is he?

JULIA: He always says the same: 'I'm a serving officer.'

MARCUS: Of course, you would expect that.

JULIA: So what was he doing at the Ministry of Defence all morning?

MARCUS: Well, he takes orders from somebody, doesn't he? His senior officers must be there...... ah.

JULIA: Carry on. His senior officers?

MARCUS: Yes. I see what you mean.

JULIA: The Barbarians run the Ministry of Defence. So what was he doing there for two hours? Reporting to his boss?

MARCUS: Well, who knows what's happened to people like him?

JULIA: This afternoon I found out. I followed him to that little square full of pine trees, just inside the Western Gate.

MARCUS: Yes....

JULIA: And there I watched him having an intense conversation, lasting nearly an hour, with Octavius and Lavinia..... you know, the two student leaders.

MARCUS: Yes, we met them at Augustus' house.

JULIA: When they'd gone, he sat there for a moment, and then got up to leave, so at that point I went over and introduced myself - as though by accident - and he told me a whole pack of lies: no, he hadn't seen anyone, he'd come to buy a book at a specialist bookshop near the square, all sorts of nonsense. Then, out of a kind of instinct, I offered him a lift back. I knew perfectly well he had his car with him, I'd followed him all the way from his flat in mine. But he accepted, without turning a hair, and all the way back to town, he pumped me about what I was doing, who I was meeting, what my plans were.

MARCUS: I see.

JULIA: He's working for them.

MARCUS: You think so?

JULIA: He must be! Look, he's carefully making contact with all the radical elements in the city, anyone who might join in to help plan the overthrow of the Barbarians. He's ticking us all off, one by one!

MARCUS: Is anyone planning to overthrow them? Really?

JULIA: What have we all been doing for the last couple of months?

MARCUS: Meeting. Talking. Complaining a lot, and getting angry.

JULIA: Far more than that, I assure you. You never see further than the end of your nose, Marcus, do you?

MARCUS: I often have difficulty seeing that far. Shall we go to bed? It's far too late to go back home.

JULIA: Well, you can stay here, if you like. Don't make any assumptions.

MARCUS: I never make any assumptions.

JULIA: What are we going to do?

MARCUS: What about?

JULIA: Captain Antony! He's selling us, one by one.

MARCUS: What do you suggest?

JULIA: Well..... There are some people I must see....

MARCUS: I'm going to get into bed. I'm dropping with tiredness.

JULIA: Do you want a drink?

MARCUS: No. Just sleep.

JULIA: I shall have one.

*Marcus walks across to an area suggesting the bedroom.*

MARCUS: I'm sure yours is the most comfortable bed I've ever slept in.

JULIA: That's not the bed. That's me.

MARCUS: Did you know that Augustus is giving up? Retiring to the country?

JULIA: Yes. Everybody knows. It's been common knowledge for a week.

*She pours herself a drink.*

MARCUS: Ah. Well. Not to me. I'd be glad to see the Barbarians overthrown. But I begin to wonder who exactly is going to do the overthrowing.

JULIA: There's no shortage of people, Marcus. It's a question of values. They think differently from us.

*He picks up a necklace.*

MARCUS: Good heavens!.... What's this?

JULIA: Oh...... The necklace?... a present. From an admirer.

*She crosses to the bedroom area.*

MARCUS: But.... it's diamonds!..... It must be worth a fortune. Who gave it to you?

JULIA: I had dinner with three press attachés the other evening.

MARCUS: Barbarians?

JULIA: Of course. What other sort of Government spokesmen are there? One of them gave me this.

MARCUS: For what?

JULIA: To sweeten me. Don't worry, that's what they're like, very vulgar, very rich. They give the men cases of vintage wine, cars. With the women it's always jewellery: the more expensive the better.

MARCUS: For God's sake don't wear it!

JULIA: I don't intend to. Sell it as soon as poss. Or put it into the bank and watch it grow.

MARCUS: Do they think they can buy you?

JULIA: If they do, they're making a big mistake. I'm much more expensive than that.....

*She moves away to replenish her drink. As she does so, the lights change and we see Marcus once again in his pool of light.*

MARCUS: I didn't stay with Julia that night after all. We made love, and I went home at about four a.m. On the way to my car - I'd had to park several streets away - I had to go under an old arch and past some derelict shops.

*The lights come up on an area representing the arch and the cardboard shanty town. Marcus crosses and participates in the events as he describes them.*

MARCUS: There have been beggars in that area for weeks, in fact, beggars in the streets are becoming quite a problem, particularly in the richer and more fashionable neighbourhoods. The police have instructions to be quite harsh with them if they make a nuisance of themselves. But in the last few weeks, there has been a rapidly increasing number of people, gathering under the arch and in the deserted shopfronts, who live in large cardboard boxes and packing cases. There's quite a shanty town growing up there now. One always goes past the area feeling rather disturbed, particularly at night. But that morning, at four a.m, I stumbled over one of them, stretched out full length on the pavement. I must have kicked him quite hard, but he didn't move, just gave to my foot like a sack. It was quite obvious he was dead - and I saw three more before I reached my car, flat out on the pavement for all to see. I hadn't been to Julia's flat for more than a week, and I had no idea things had come to this pass. I looked down at the first one. I thought he must have been murdered. But when I turned him over, it was quite clear what he'd died of. Starvation.

*Marcus moves across the stage to another pool of light.*

MARCUS: During the next few months that too became commonplace. Street-cleaning squads were sent out at first light to clear away the night's tally of dead to the mortuaries, twenty or thirty of them some mornings, I was told...... Two months after I saw the first corpse in the streets of our once-beautiful city, the Government dropped its bombshell. I was at a crisis meeting with Adrian the morning the news broke....

*The lights come up on Adrian's office in the theatre. Sounds of conversations and phone bells ringing from the outer office, general atmosphere of business. Marcus goes directly into the scene.*

ADRIAN: .... I tell you, Marcus, another three months like we've just had, and I shall have to close. People just aren't coming to the theatre....

MARCUS: It's too expensive, when you put the prices up last time....

ADRIAN: What else could I do? With my income cut by a third? As a matter of fact, I'm thinking of putting them up again...

MARCUS: What? That'll be suicide, surely?

ADRIAN: If it were, I wouldn't be doing it. The fact is, the audience is changing. We're getting more and more Barbarians coming, less and less of the old audience...

MARCUS: I noticed the last time I was in.

ADRIAN: And I suspect that if we put the prices up even higher, we'd get even more of them. These people are very vulgar at heart. If it were cheaper they wouldn't come.

MARCUS: But the ordinary people of the city might.

ADRIAN: Well to Hell with the ordinary people of the city! They have no money to spend on theatre these days.

MARCUS: Then is it really worth all this effort? Why not shut up shop now?

ADRIAN: Shut up shop? My dear boy, I have kept this theatre going for more than thirty years, through worse times than this!

MARCUS: But what for?

ADRIAN: What for? For itself, of course! Theatre is its own justification.

MARCUS: Oh, is it? I thought it was a way of speaking to people.

ADRIAN: It is, of course! It's always been that....

MARCUS: The way you're talking, you'd do anything at all to keep open.

ADRIAN: I would! I have done! Don't talk to me about the politics of the thing, Marcus, because I won't listen. I'm an unashamed whore for my profession, and have been since I could toddle. The theatre has no politics. It's a performing space, people perform within it...

MARCUS: But you used to perform for the people of this city, I remember because I was there, I was one of them when I was a young man. Whatever the great issues of the day, within months they would be dramatised on your stage!

ADRIAN: Yes, yes, dear boy, but that was last year. Tomorrow, next week, next year, that's what matters in the theatre, not the past!

MARCUS: We're both working a fourteen hour day here, and for what? To make the Barbarians laugh?

ADRIAN: So, do you want to make them cry, do you want to confront them with the great issues of the day? They'd stop coming, cut my subsidy and close my theatre. And what good would that do? Much more to the point, find out what they want, and give them more of it1

MARCUS: Well, that's your ambition, Adrian, not mine.

ADRIAN: When the times change, the theatre changes with them. That's how it survives.

MARCUS: I'll just hunt out the money, and keep my mouth shut....

ADRIAN: Yes!

*A Secretary puts her head in.*

SECRETARY: Julia here to see you, shall I let her in?

ADRIAN: Julia? What's she doing here? Are you expecting her?

MARCUS: No.

ADRIAN: Neither am I.

MARCUS: Nobody ever is. It's one of her most valuable talents.

ADRIAN: Yes, let her in

*But Julia bustles in before the Secretary has time to invite her.*

JULIA: Have you two been listening to the news?

ADRIAN: No, why?

MARCUS: What happened?

JULIA: At lunch time today the Government announced two new bills, one for the alleviation of unemployment, the other for the rehousing of the homeless.

ADRIAN: Well, that's good isn't it? They say that one in five is out of work, and the number of beggars and people living rough in the streets is becoming a national disgrace....

MARCUS: What are they doing?

JULIA: All the unemployed, and the homeless, are going to be given free housing, food, and jobs.... in return for unpaid labour. Special centres are going to be built where they can all live together. These special centres will have barbed wire perimeters, for everybody's safety! Those who work outside, will go in and out under guard.

MARCUS: Good heavens, that sounds more like....

JULIA: It sounds like what it is. They're bringing back slavery!

*Blackout or freeze.*

# END OF ACT ONE

# ACT TWO

*A group of men and women, dressed in drab hessian jackets and trousers, moves slowly across the stage. They are chained to each other at the wrists. An armed guard walks with them. Marcus comes on stage, watching them. As he does, the lights multiply the figures into many hundreds, like an endless field of mirrors.*

MARCUS: It certainly solved the problem. Within weeks there were no more derelicts on the streets, production rose, and profits soared. There were plenty of people quite willing to say that slavery was a drastic solution, certainly, but it did seem that the Barbarians had got it right. At every other dinner-party you met two or three well-heeled chaps with overpainted wives who said that you might not agree with the morality of the thing, but when it came to solving problems, the Barbarians had got us licked.

*The slaves disappear, and Marcus walks forward into his pool of light.*

MARCUS: Three weeks later, I got an appointment with the whizz-kid, Tarquin. I had written to him as soon as Augustus mentioned his name, and received a dismissive reply, so I was apprehensive at being summoned to meet him that same evening, in his office at the top of a tower of black glass that had risen in the city financial district, like a slab of memorial marble in a cemetery. There were security guards on the door, with pistols on their belts.

*As Marcus crosses the stage a Security Guard emerges from the darkness and stops him.*

GUARD: Name?

MARCUS: Marcus. I've an appointment to see Tarquin.

GUARD: Wait please.

*The Guard moves back into the darkness.*

MARCUS: He went inside his office, and there was a long pause. I was quite unable to see what they were doing. It was like waiting at a frontier crossing into a hostile country.

*The Guard re-emerges into the light.*

GUARD: Take the lift on the left. That will take you direct to the top floor. You'll be met there...

*The Guard goes offstage.*

MARCUS: The lift was fast and silent, and the office....

*The lights come up on the opposite side of the stage, revealing Tarquin, at his impressive desk. A group of figures is seated on a long sofa, unlit as yet, and visible only as silhouettes.*

MARCUS: ...was enormous, glass all the way round, with all the lights of the city visible, like the camp fires of an invading army. Tarquin was seated what seemed miles away, a small rat-like man, with a face that never seemed to smile even when it was amused. There were other people there too, sitting in shadow. I couldn't see who they were.

TARQUIN: Come in, Marcus, sit down.

MARCUS: Thank you...

*There is a longish pause, as Tarquin turns over pages on his desk.*

TARQUIN: You wrote a letter. Three and-a-half months ago.

MARCUS: Yes... I was hoping you might...

TARQUIN: I have it in front of me. There was no prospect of doing anything when it arrived. Now there is.

MARCUS: Ah, I'm very glad...

TARQUIN: You need not say anything for the moment. Unless I ask you to speak.

MARCUS: No.

*Another pause. More paper turning.*

TARQUIN: I remember your letter, of course. It was too long. One paragraph is enough.

MARCUS: Yes. I'm sure.

TARQUIN: But.... I am interested in the theatre. I always have been.

*A pause.*

TARQUIN: You have money of your own. Why don't you use that?

MARCUS: It's all tied up, in property and investments. I wasn't asked to put money into the theatre, merely to work for it.

TARQUIN: What investments?

MARCUS: Nothing of any interest. My father made all the arrangements, and I've hardly changed them at all.

TARQUIN: That's very foolish of you. The market has changed completely in the last twenty years. You've probably lost a great deal of money.

MARCUS: No doubt. I'm not much interested. I have enough.

TARQUIN: Not very good credentials: to come asking for money when you manage your own so inefficiently.

MARCUS: Not at all. I'm prudent enough to ask you to use your money without endangering mine. That's how I have managed to live comfortably on my income for twenty years.

*Subdued laughter, harsh and grating.*

MARCUS: You must have had a purpose inviting me here after ignoring me for three months. What is it?

TARQUIN: We think your theatre is interesting. Getting more interesting all the time.

MARCUS: Who are 'we'?

TARQUIN: Never mind that for the moment. If it is likely to progress in the same way as it has been doing, we might well put up some money.

MARCUS: I'm glad to hear that.

TARQUIN: These gentlemen represent a consortium of business interests I have put together for other purposes. For the right project they might put up a substantial sum...

*The lights come upon the Barbarians seated on the sofa.*

MARCUS: And there they were, five Barbarians, sitting on that huge sofa. These were the people who had put my ancestors' heads on poles, and burned all the great libraries of the city - and now they were sitting in the same room, in their bulging, tightly-buttoned suits and striped ties, and polished black shoes, like hooves, and I suddenly realised the difference. Money. Their pockets were crammed with it, every spare seam or flap thick with wallets and credit cards, or stuffed with wads of notes. These were Barbarians all right, descendants of the old destroyers, but unlike their forefathers, they were very, very rich, riding that sofa on a warm cushion of cash!

*One of the Barbarians speaks to Marcus. He has a very smooth, plausible, public school voice.*

BARBARIAN: We thought, for the right play, or the right programme of plays, we might be prepared to be very generous indeed.

MARCUS: What is the right kind of play?

BARBARIAN: Personally, I've always been devoted to the drama of the Greeks. You look surprised..... Barbarians are not supposed to appreciate such things, I know, but the fact is that we do, some of us. You're out of date to think otherwise. The one about the King who marries his mother, for instance. I'd love to see that again.

MARCUS: **Oedipus.** By Sophocles.

BARBARIAN: That's the one. Going to bed with his mother after murdering his father, as I remember it. And quite unaware of the fact! That has all kinds of possibilities. I can think of a great many people who would come to see that.

MARCUS: That doesn't actually happen in the play, of course.

BARBARIAN: But we don't want to be academic about these things do we? They're living theatre, not museum pieces. I'm sure there are a good many young directors who would love to re-interpret plays like that, in line with modern taste.

MARCUS: Yes, I'm sure there are....

SECOND BARBARIAN: And, at the end of it, if my memory serves me right, he is blinded!

BARBARIAN: That's right, he is !

SECOND BARBARIAN: With two ornamental pins! And he comes on stage with his eyes streaming blood and pus.

BARBARIAN: Yes. Blinded.

SECOND BARBARIAN: That's right. Fascinating!

BARBARIAN: Real theatre!

SECOND BARBARIAN Absolutely!

BARBARIAN: You know, I'm sure there'd be a great many people who would be very excited to see a play like that, aren't you?

MARCUS: Well...

SECOND BARBARIAN: Absolutely! You can't beat these old things, can you? They knew what people want, in those days. Something to keep them riveted to their seats.

BARBARIAN: Real theatre. Real!

SECOND BARBARIAN: Absolutely!

MARCUS: It was the longest hour of my life. When it was over, I half stumbled to the lift, as though I had been blinded. I walked straight past the guard with my head down, convinced he was about to arrest me, and when I got outside I was completely disorientated, as though I was a stranger in a city I'd never seen before. But The Palatine Hotel is only a block away from Tarquin's office, and even that vulgarity seemed civilising after an evening spent among Barbarians.

> *The lights fade on Tarquin and the Barbarians as Marcus begins his speech, and come up on Captain Antony on the other side of the stage, in the bar at The Palatine Hotel. He has a bottle of wine on the table and two glasses. He has a little wine in his own glass, but the bottle is more or less untouched.*

CAPTAIN ANTONY: Marcus! Won't you come and join me?

MARCUS: Oh... er.

CAPTAIN ANTONY: You look as if you could do with a drink.

> *Somewhat reluctantly Marcus crosses to join him, as Captain Antony pours him a glass of wine.*

MARCUS: I could do with a good many. I've just been closeted with them for nearly an hour.

CAPTAIN ANTONY: So even the bar at The Palatine seems acceptable.

MARCUS: Anywhere at all. Anywhere that sells alcohol.

CAPTAIN ANTONY: You notice we don't ask who anymore.

MARCUS: No need to. Who else?

CAPTAIN ANTONY: Indeed. (*They both drink.*) I was rather hoping I'd see you, as a matter of fact.

MARCUS: Oh... Were you?

CAPTAIN ANTONY: We've hardly met since you began your great adventure with Adrian.

MARCUS: Oh. Is that what it is!

CAPTAIN ANTONY: I wondered how you were getting on..... This can't have been the first time.

MARCUS: No. But never for so long before.

CAPTAIN ANTONY: What do you make of them?

MARCUS: (*Nervously drinking*) Why do you want to know?

CAPTAIN ANTONY: Because I find it interesting, the different ways people react - now that we know them, and are beginning to get used to them.

MARCUS: I'm not getting used to them.

CAPTAIN ANTONY: Well, to some degree. Some people.

MARCUS: What do you find interesting?

CAPTAIN ANTONY: Well - for instance - if you gave someone a plate of vomit to eat or a glass of piss to drink, they would retch, I imagine, almost all of them.

MARCUS: Naturally.

CAPTAIN ANTONY: But some people, eventually, would eat and drink. They'd hold their noses, and their stomachs would heave. But they would do it.

MARCUS: Not me.

CAPTAIN ANTONY: Perhaps.... Are you sure?

MARCUS: Quite sure.

CAPTAIN ANTONY: I'd like to believe you. But I do have this feeling, that in the long run.....

MARCUS: What?

CAPTAIN ANTONY: Most people would eat the vomit, and drink the piss. If they were told it was the right thing to do and everybody was doing it. Or if the price was right.

MARCUS: I wouldn't. I'm sure.

CAPTAIN ANTONY: I'm talking in metaphors, of course.

MARCUS: Yes. Of course...

CAPTAIN ANTONY: They are rather more digestible than actual vomit or piss.

MARCUS: You've lost me, I'm afraid.

CAPTAIN ANTONY: It doesn't matter. Just a game. Something must have displeased you in there, by the way you came out.

MARCUS: There is something disgusting about them. Not externally. They're more or less like us these days. Deep inside them. Something inhuman, unhuman. You know what it is? They laugh at the wrong things. You should never trust people who laugh at the wrong things.

CAPTAIN ANTONY: What are the wrong things?

MARCUS: Oh don't ask me, I'm no philosopher. Pain.

CAPTAIN ANTONY: Indeed.

MARCUS: I was a little disturbed by my own behaviour too.

CAPTAIN ANTONY: In what way?

MARCUS: I'm not a brash person. I think I can say that, with some honesty. Too insignificant.

CAPTAIN ANTONY: No.

MARCUS: And yet, I heard myself saying the kind of rubbishy, aggressive things I knew would go down well with them. I was ashamed of the crudity of what I was saying. But they loved it. I didn't like that feeling.

ANTONY: No one does. Of course, the really interesting speculation - I'm not talking about your mild personality change - is how far will people go. Is there a limit?

MARCUS: The fact is, we should have as little to do with them as we can. Only meet civilised people.

CAPTAIN ANTONY: As we are both doing. Provided we can be quite sure who they are.

*He laughs softly.*

MARCUS: Who were you waiting for?

CAPTAIN ANTONY: I wasn't waiting for anyone.

MARCUS: But the wine. You'd hardly drunk any. You had two glasses.

CAPTAIN ANTONY: Well. I'm a naturally sociable person.

*Antony drinks, and Marcus rises from him into his pool of light as the lights fade on Antony.*

MARCUS: As I left him, I suddenly had the terrified feeling he had known about my appointment, and had been waiting for me there, with the bottle ready open. I remembered what Julia had said about him. And I suddenly felt as though I had stepped into a cold store, full of hanging carcases, and the sweat was freezing on my face.

*The pool of light fades and Marcus goes offstage. On the other side of the stage the lights come up on Adrian's office, where Adrian is talking to the young actor.*

ACTOR: Adrian, I can't tell you how grateful I am, really...

ADRIAN: Don't say another word about it, dear boy, it's my pleasure to keep you on the books.

ACTOR: It was a dreadful blow, after what had seemed such a good season...

ADRIAN: Don't ever confuse art with commerce, dear heart, or you'll get yourself into all kinds of trouble. Keep them in separate compartments, and you'll be surprised how much you'll thrive.

ACTOR: Yes, I see that now.

ADRIAN: Your talent wasn't ever in question. We all know what a furry little genius you are, and what a bushy-tailed career you're going to have. It was just that I couldn't afford you, or indeed anybody. And now I can.

ACTOR: Well, I must say, it's really thrilling...

ADRIAN: Good. You have signed both copies?

ACTOR: Yes.

ADRIAN: That's the way.

ACTOR: Do you know what we're going to do yet?

ADRIAN: Oh, it's all very amorphous as yet, dear boy, very cloudy. But one or two things are beginning to emerge. We might possibly do a Greekie.

ACTOR: Oh, how wonderful! I adore Greek tragedy!

ADRIAN: Of course you do, everybody does. Fortunately for us. I'll see you in a month dear boy, best frock, nice deodorant, ready to work.

*He is shuffling the Actor offstage. Marcus is lurking on the edge of the light.*

ACTOR: Oh certainly, Adrian, thank you again....

ADRIAN: Come in, Marcus.

*The Actor goes. Marcus comes into the light*

ADRIAN: Don't lurk over by the bookshelf. It's only full of unsolicited plays, and nobody ever reads them.

MARCUS: I meant to come and see you yesterday, straight after the meeting, but I got waylaid by Antony. Then I went home to bed.

ADRIAN: So. How did you get on? With the whizz-kid?

MARCUS: He's terrifying.

ADRIAN: Oh yes, he's that all right. Most talented people are. For instance, you frighten the life out of me!

MARCUS: Me? I wouldn't terrify a woolly rabbit.

ADRIAN: Don't you believe it. You uncommitted people who don't give a damn are the most dangerous of the lot.

MARCUS: Oh, really?

ADRIAN: Look at it from my point of view. If I can't buy you with money or with art, what can I buy you with?

MARCUS: You can't buy me with anything. I'm not for sale.

ADRIAN: Exactly. Terrifying!

MARCUS: Well.

ADRIAN: So, what did you make of them?

MARCUS: Nothing very new. Barbarians are Barbarians. Some of them can be very charming. It's what they believe that's uncivilised, and you can't ever quite get around that, however much small talk you make.

ADRIAN: Well. Social niceties apart, do you think they are going to give us any money?

MARCUS: I think they might. But at a price.

ADRIAN: No money is ever free, Marcus. You always have to pay for it, one way or another.

MARCUS: That's what I'm afraid of.

ADRIAN: You mustn't be afraid, dear boy, don't ever be afraid in the theatre, or you are done for! I have a feeling that all kinds of new possibilities are opening up for us at the moment. They may be strange, alien even, not what we think of as the normal way of working. But every now and then the theatre makes one of those lurches forward, or a sideways jump into a totally new country. A new way of doing things, which means new values, and new methods. It's always terrifically exciting when that happens. And I think we may be standing on the verge of one of those leaps forward now!

MARCUS: To what? Barbarian theatre? From the way they were talking that's what they'd like.

ADRIAN: Not at all, dear boy, not at all. Don't forget, we make theatre, not them. They only pay for it. We do what we want, and convince them it's what they meant all along. But we must keep our minds open, so that new things can enter, that's the point.

MARCUS: I see.

ADRIAN: That's how theatre has grown, from the beginning.

Influences feed into us from all sides, and we assimilate them, and make them our own. The whole history of culture is like that. A continuous process of transformation. Nothing static, ever! The audience always dictates what we do in the long run. They hurl their concerns at us, like raw, unrefined chunks of experience. And we turn them into art.

MARCUS: Jolly good. Sounds wonderful. The raw experience they hurled at me yesterday wasn't so much unrefined as positively stinking. But I assume you know what you're doing.

ADRIAN: Of course I do, dear boy! Let me tell you something - a word in your shell-like ear... I've already had a word with Tarquin on the phone. Quite a long chat. And you did well dear boy. You did very well. They were impressed.

MARCUS: Well, I'm very happy to hear that, Adrian. I suppose if you can impress a Barbarian, you can impress anybody.

*Marcus goes offstage, as the illumination closes round Adrian. He pours himself a large glass of wine. He is tense and sweating.*

ADRIAN: This isn't going to be easy. ( *He drinks* ) By God no, it's not going to be easy. I know the chance I'm taking better than anyone else does. But it's the lifebelt, or drown. And I'm not going to drown, not after all this time. Keep the art in one pocket, the money in the other, that's the secret. Give them what they want to start with, and gradually civilise them. That's what art is for, isn't it? To make people more civilised? Whatever point they start from....

*He takes another long glass of wine as the lights fade on him. There is darkness for a few moments, with the suggestion of ominous disturbing music. When the lights come up again we are in Julia's flat. The door opens and Marcus enters.*

MARCUS: Julia, where are you...? Are you in..?

JULIA: In the bathroom.

MARCUS: Well hurry up and get out, I think I may very well want to be sick.

JULIA: Where have you been...? The last night?

MARCUS: Yes. I had to, I was absolutely compelled to by Adrian, who said he'd lose all the money, if the man who had arranged it wasn't there. Which isn't true. He just wanted me to share complicity in the crime.

*Julia enters from the bathroom.*

MARCUS: I've never been so disgusted in my life. I feel filthy at the thought.

JULIA: What happened?

MARCUS: The first act was its usual squalid spectacle, Oedipus and Jocasta fucking on the sofa, I'm really getting quite used to that now. There were the usual two or three couples who started making love in the stalls, and a dozen or so masturbating more or less surreptitiously. I hardly know why they bother. Doing it every day on stage for a month, and faking it on matinée days, the actors are really beginning to look thoroughly bored with the whole process. But it still seems to work the audience up. Can't beat professionals, can you?

JULIA: But tonight must have been different.

MARCUS: It was horrible. Every word the poor man said was followed by a kind of prurient shudder of expectation. When he went off, just before the blinding, the silence was quite electrifying There was a pause, and the Chorus started speaking, and then there was the most agonised shuddering scream from backstage, and a great buzz went round the audience - no one listened to what the Chorus was saying at all. Just that dreadful moaning from the wings. They had doctors in attendance, but they had been asked not to touch him till after the final scene. Just to check that he could still get onto the stage.

JULIA: And did he?

MARCUS: Oh yes. He was tremendous. Gave the performance of his life. Fell down the steps half-way down, terrific laugh that got. Sounds silly to say it, but his performance was full of real pain. He got a terrific reception at the curtain call. Then he was rushed straight off to the hospital for the wounds to be treated. There wasn't much blood actually, not half as much as we usually have with stage blood. There was a bit of disappointment about that. You could hardly see anything at all.

JULIA: Except he was blinded.

MARCUS: Yes. Completely. Couldn't see a thing.

JULIA: With an ornamental brooch.

MARCUS: A very small one. And it was sterilised. They were afraid if they used the sort of brooch the text describes, it might pierce the brain and kill him. Spoil the play.

JULIA: God!

*A pause.*

MARCUS: I saw Adrian afterwards, with Tarquin, and the whole cackling bunch of Barbarian sponsors, nearly bursting out of their buttons, they'd enjoyed themselves so much.

JULIA: What did he say?

MARCUS: He was absolutely drained, his face the colour of bad milk. He got me in a corner and said 'You don't have to say anything to me, dear boy, and I only have one thing to say to you. Charging £500 per seat tonight, gala prices, with an audience ninety per cent Barbarian, we've taken over £200,000. Enough to keep us going, with real drama, for the best part of next year.' I said nothing and left. The rest of them are at a huge cast party. Except for the poor devil who played Oedipus. He's in hospital.

JULIA: How did they persuade him to do it?

MARCUS: You can always get an actor from somewhere to play anything. He's a good middle-aged fellow with a lot of unrecognised talent, who's never really been given the big chance. He said to me last week, 'I get to play one of the greatest of all parts, for a month, at a very large salary. And after that, well, there's plenty of parts for blind actors. I shall become the best-known Tieresias of my generation.'

JULIA: Actors are extraordinary people. You can't help admiring them.

MARCUS: Are they? They'll do anything at all for the chance to act, most of them. Is that so very different from doing anything for money?

JULIA: Yes. I think it is.

MARCUS: Well. I'm too tired to argue about it. Let's go to bed.

JULIA: No, not yet. There's something I have to talk to you about, first.

MARCUS: Oh, really? What?

JULIA: Something important.

MARCUS: Couldn't you have picked some other time?

JULIA: No. I didn't know for sure till today.

MARCUS: What?

JULIA: Pour yourself a drink

MARCUS: Is it that serious?

JULIA: It's serious.

MARCUS: About what?

JULIA: Our friend Captain Antony

MARCUS: (*Wearily*) Ah. How did I guess?

JULIA: You've heard me talk of.... other people... Other people I must see.

MARCUS: Yes.

JULIA: You've never wondered who they are?

MARCUS: Yes, frequently, but there are certain questions I make a point of not asking. Particularly about you. Ignorance is a blessed state that leads to peace.

JULIA: Since the beginning, even before they came, the Barbarians I mean, I've been in contact with an undercover revolutionary group: no, call a spade a spade - a terrorist group. A group of ultras who are prepared to use the most violent means.

MARCUS: Are looking forward to it, in fact. Why did you want to meet such people? They exist in every society, we all know that.

JULIA: Because I was so.... appalled by what was happening. I couldn't endure the thought of the Barbarians being here. It seemed that anything would be justified to remove them.

MARCUS: But you don't think that any longer?

JULIA: I don't know what I think. If I thought the murder of half a dozen prominent Barbarians would do the job....? But I don't. There are too many of them now.

MARCUS: What does this have to do with Captain Antony?

JULIA: I've become more and more suspicious that he is selling us. Me. And you too. All of us.

MARCUS: He wouldn't get a very good price for me.

JULIA: Marcus, it isn't funny!

MARCUS: No, it isn't funny.

JULIA: We know he is based at the Ministry of Defence, and reports there regularly. We also know that some people do disappear, and that open opponents of the regime are in danger. Why did Augustus retire so suddenly to his farm?

MARCUS: He'd had enough. Claudia persuaded him.

JULIA: Or was he threatened? Get out, or else?

MARCUS: I don't know.

JULIA: If Antony is compiling dossiers on us all, how soon before we disappear, or are invited to retire to the country?

MARCUS: It's all supposition, Julia, no facts. Though, now I come to think of it...

JULIA: What?

MARCUS: He was waiting for me after my first meeting with Tarquin. I'm almost sure he was. And he did ask me all kinds of odd questions.

JULIA: Well, today, there was more. I went to see... the people I told you about. They're still there. There'll be action from them, eventually, when they're ready.

MARCUS: No doubt.

JULIA: They've had a visit from Captain Antony, too. Long discussions, as though to help in the setting up of a revolutionary conspiracy. And, like me, they were very suspicious. I told them what I knew.

MARCUS: And?

JULIA: They are ninety per cent convinced he's an agent. Softening us all up for the knife.

MARCUS: What about the other ten per cent?

JULIA: They'll probably kill him.

MARCUS: Only probably?

JULIA: That's where we come in.

MARCUS: We don't come in at all. I certainly don't. It's nothing to do with me.

JULIA: Yes it is Marcus.

MARCUS: Whatever it is, I won't do it.

JULIA: Not to prove him innocent? Because we don't know for certain, do we?.... Not to keep coming to this flat when you feel like it?

MARCUS: That's a pretty disgusting thing to say.

JULIA: We need to know, Marcus. Our lives may be at stake.

MARCUS: What do you mean, to prove his innocence?

JULIA: These people were ready to execute him on the spot. Suspicion is enough for them where informers are concerned. I argued that we couldn't be sure. But that I would find out. Set up a kind of test: and then report to them. Your part in the plan will....

MARCUS: No, no, I have no part....

JULIA: You have to, Marcus, you must! You have money, and a safe house in the country. We'll both go and stay there, and we'll invite him to meet you. He won't know I'm there. I shall arrive secretly, after he does. The actual test will be up to you.

MARCUS: Why should I? I never take part in anything.

JULIA: This time you must: for me, and for yourself.

MARCUS: What do you want me to do at my safe house in the country?

JULIA: Pour yourself another drink, and I'll tell you. Do you carry a gun?

MARCUS: What?

JULIA: A gun.

MARCUS: Of course not.

JULIA: You'd better borrow mine. If he is a secret-service man, he's sure to be armed, and if you put him on the spot, it might be wise if you were.

MARCUS: How long have you carried a gun?

JULIA: Since slavery came back there are at least three gangs of runaways at large in the city. They rob and murder anyone who looks at all well-off, especially women. It's class-war on the streets. Much safer to be armed.

MARCUS: Well Julia, you keep your little pop-gun to yourself. If Antony pulls anything, possessing that will certainly encourage him to shoot me. And I wouldn't be able to shoot anything, except maybe my own foot.

JULIA: Well. Suit yourself.

MARCUS: Tell me about this test. I'm not promising anything.

JULIA: You are, Marcus. You don't have any choice in the matter.

*The lights fade on Julia's flat, as Marcus comes into his pool of light.*

MARCUS: Julia certainly moved fast when she wanted to get something done. And this time she seemed to be driven by something like panic. Within a week it was fixed. I had even spoken to Antony on the 'phone - Julia had briefed me what to say - inviting him to stay with me for a weekend in the country. I told him I had something very important to discuss with him, that concerned the safety of all of us. He seemed very open and willing, not the least bit suspicious. I was quite terrified at the prospect, not at all sure I was actor enough to carry it through. We fixed a date, two weeks ahead. But on the Wednesday beforehand, I got an urgent phone call from Adrian, who was positively bubbling with high spirits. He told me I had to come into the theatre that very afternoon, for an important meeting with a new colleague.

*The lights come up on Adrian's office.*

ADRIAN: Come in, dear boy, come in and share the good news.

MARCUS: I didn't think there ever was any, in this business.

ADRIAN: This time there is. Sit down, dear boy, and prepare to rest on your laurels.

MARCUS: Mine?

ADRIAN: I've had several talks with Tarquin during the last week. He was very pleased with the **Oedipus** gala-night. He said all his clients really enjoyed themselves.

MARCUS: Rather publicly, some of them.

ADRIAN: Now don't be stuffy, dear boy, things change; moral standards vary - autre temps, autre moeurs, or whatever it is. It isn't the first time that sort of thing's gone on in the theatre.

MARCUS: That's what you meant by openness to new ideas is it?

ADRIAN: Part of it, yes. If it has to be.

MARCUS: I'm so glad Tarquin is pleased.

ADRIAN: He was more than pleased. He reckoned that single night was probably worth nearly a million pounds in business to his consortium.

MARCUS: What they call greasing the wheels of commerce.

ADRIAN: Absolutely! The point is, he is very keen that the association between us should continue, and be placed on a more permanent footing.

MARCUS: Why don't we just open a brothel, Adrian? It would be much less trouble.

ADRIAN: But not half as satisfying. Don't be naïve. If we play our cards right, this theatre's finances will be secure for the next ten years. I know we pay a price, but isn't it worth paying? A few bad nights and a whole year of achievement? Now don't argue, just listen!... I've brought you here to meet someone. My new assistant director, entirely funded by Tarquin and his consortium! Come in, dear boy, show yourself to Marcus. We're all going to be working together on some very exciting projects. Let me introduce my young protégé, Cloten.

> *Cloten enters, about twenty-three, dark-haired, rather ugly, wearing fashionable workman's clothes and hobnailed boots, looking as though he's just come off a building site, or down a painter's ladder, except that the clothes have come from a smart man's shop, not Millets.*

CLOTEN: Hallo, Marcus, nice to know you.

ADRIAN: Cloten is a very bright young director indeed. He is going to work very closely with both of us on the whole programme, but with special responsibility for the gala evenings.

CLOTEN: I have this concept, Marcus, let me share it with you, of the incredible one-off, the unmissable event. **Oedipus** was one such evening, and I plan that **Richard the Third** will be the next.

MARCUS: Really ?

CLOTEN: I've been working on **Hamlet** and **Lear**, even **Antony and Cleopatra**. But Hamlet talks too much after he's been stabbed, Lear dies for no apparent reason, and you can't possibly rely on a snake bite. **Richard** is safe though. Four or five well-armed knights should be enough to do the job.

MARCUS: I see. And where will you find the actor to play the King?

CLOTEN: Oh, don't get me wrong, he'll have a fighting chance, and there'll be two alternative endings. We'll get him well trained too, so he'll make a real scrap of it. The uncertainty will be one of the big selling points. I think we'll probably be able to charge a £1,000 per ticket for that concept, don't you ?

MARCUS: Why ask me? I'm nothing to do with it.

ADRIAN: Of course you are, dear boy, your role is crucial in the whole thing. Without you we'd never have been able to start at all.

MARCUS: Well somehow, Adrian, you must stagger on without me. I resign, as from now.....

ADRIAN: Marcus, this is ridiculous...! Why are you doing such a very foolish thing?

MARCUS: Because **Richard the Third** has never been a favourite play of mine. What other possible reason could there be?

*Marcus sweeps out.*

CLOTEN: Maybe he'd prefer **Macbeth**?

*Adrian winces at Cloten's solecism, and the lights fade on his office, as Marcus comes into the pool of light. As he speaks we hear the pastoral sounds of Marcus' villa, and the lights gradually come up on the scene, casting gobo patterns on the edges of the central area which represents the villa.*

MARCUS: My villa is spacious and comfortable, with arched loggias and cool tiled floors. It stands in a countryside of low steep hills, patterned with vineyards and olive groves, and lined with clumps of cypresses, which, on warm summer evenings, look like rows of black candles pointing to the sky. The sunsets are magnificent behind the hills all through summer and autumn, and to sit out in the garden at ten o'clock, with a glass of cool white wine from my own vineyards, listening to the evening sound of the cicadas, is the nearest I will ever get to Paradise. Antony arrived at lunch-time on Saturday, and we spent a very pleasant day together. On Sunday, as arranged with Julia, I took him for a long walk, while she arrived and got herself settled in. On Sunday evening after dinner, as we poured the first brandies, it couldn't be postponed any longer.

*Captain Antony enters as Marcus pours the brandies.*

CAPTAIN ANTONY: You asked me here for a purpose, Marcus. I think it's about time you told me what it is.

MARCUS: I asked you here because, through Julia, I've come to think of you as a good friend. And to good friends you like to do favours.

CAPTAIN ANTONY: What favours?

MARCUS: This is the most beautiful villa for some miles around, and the vineyards and olive groves all belong to me, pretty well as far as you can see. There are other estates too, and property in the city All inherited, of course. None of the energy that acquired all this was mine.

CAPTAIN ANTONY: Very pleasant. What is it to do with me?

MARCUS: We have talked together about what has happened since the Barbarians came. We have gone to the same protest meetings, had earnest conversations with the same people. But I have gradually come to see... after all, they have been here for some time now.

CAPTAIN ANTONY: What have you come to see?

MARCUS: Where my own best interests lie. As a rich man, and a landowner, the Barbarians, in a very real sense, speak for me. I may not like what they do too much, but it certainly reinforces my own position. To be brief... I have come to support them and what they are doing. More than that. I have become a passionate advocate of their cause.

CAPTAIN ANTONY: Every man's opinions are his own.

MARCUS: No, I haven't made myself clear. My conviction is such that I am prepared to do anything I can to ensure their continued triumph in this country. But I also regard you as a friend.

CAPTAIN ANTONY: I'm flattered.

MARCUS: I know you are a serving officer, and I assume you are in Intelligence. I also know that you are secretly working to encourage the revolutionary overthrow of the Barbarian regime.

CAPTAIN ANTONY: You seem to know a great deal.

MARCUS: Well, it's quite obvious, isn't it. I know you have been making a point of seeking out all the most subversive elements in society, with the aim of uniting them into some kind of revolutionary coalition. I know that to be a fact.

CAPTAIN ANTONY: And?

MARCUS: If I were to make a brief phone call, you would be arrested within two hours. But I prefer to make you a proposition. Because I like you, and consider you my friend.

CAPTAIN ANTONY: Very gallant of you.

MARCUS: I will buy all the information you have gathered about subversive groups and people who intend to overthrow the Barbarians. I will buy your whole dossier, for a very considerable sum. It will be enough for you to live in one of the obscurer provinces of the Empire, or abroad, if you prefer that. I will do nothing with the dossier till you have had time to make yourself scarce, to go, and to cover your tracks. A month, shall we say? I shall then hand it over to the relevant authorities, with my recommendation for immediate action.

CAPTAIN ANTONY: Supposing I reject your offer?

MARCUS: There is a letter already at the Ministry. It won't be opened for three days. If you agree to my proposal, and if I am still safe enough to do so, the letter will be withdrawn.

CAPTAIN ANTONY: A neat little trap.

MARCUS: Very neat.

CAPTAIN ANTONY: Shall we have another brandy?

MARCUS: Why not?

CAPTAIN ANTONY: Marcus, ( *Moving to the brandy* ) you are an awfully nice fellow. But you are a rotten actor, and a truly lousy conspirator.

MARCUS: I beg your pardon?

CAPTAIN ANTONY: I happen to know you have not become a convert to Barbarism. I have a longish folder on you too, after all. I happen to know also that you have walked out of Adrian's theatre in disgust, because it has become a plaything of the Barbarians. And I can recognise Julia's clumsy hand when I see it. So shall we forget all that nonsense, and try to establish why I am really here?

MARCUS: I really don't know what to say...

CAPTAIN ANTONY: I suppose Julia is here too, listening in to all this?

MARCUS: I.... suppose she is.

CAPTAIN ANTONY: And that you cooked up this ridiculous story between you as a kind of test of my motives. To find out what I was doing, and whose side I was really on?

MARCUS: Something like that.

CAPTAIN ANTONY: Well, Marcus, I am an intelligence officer, I have been for some years. And I can assure you, you are going to have to do a great deal better than that.

MARCUS: I'm afraid I lacked conviction from the start.

CAPTAIN ANTONY: I became an intelligence officer, because I believed in the democracy, passionately, and knew it had to be defended with all the weapons a state has at its disposal. Undercover work was part of it. The just society would always need that, if it was to defend itself from the unjust.

MARCUS: But the democracy lost. The Barbarians are here.

CAPTAIN ANTONY: It abjectly surrendered itself, as though the task of creating justice and equality for all was finally beyond its powers. But I don't believe that. Immediately at the take-over, the Barbarian security chiefs vetted all the junior officers... and they trusted me. I impressed them how devoted I was to the cause of the secure state, whoever was running it. I volunteered to conduct an immediate investigation into subversive activity among all known opponents of Barbarian rule.

MARCUS: And?

CAPTAIN ANTONY: Well.... I was doing the exact opposite. I was searching diligently to see how best to put together a coalition that might have some chance of bringing the Barbarians down. I fed them lots of spuriously convincing stuff to keep them happy. I do have a dossier, on all of us. Not a very inspiring document. They have seen not one word of it, nor will they.

MARCUS: Thank God for that. There are people who want to kill you....

CAPTAIN ANTONY: Yes. A good many people. At least two organised groups, whose names and backgrounds I could give you in detail. Julia has been in contact with one of them for more than a year.

MARCUS: What are you going to do?

CAPTAIN ANTONY: It started out, my little investigation, as political, undercover work. But it soon became something more than that. More of a philosophical enquiry.

MARCUS: What do you mean?

CAPTAIN ANTONY: It became clear very quickly that there wasn't a hope in hell of putting together any kind of revolutionary conspiracy that would have a chance of success. The Barbarians had been invited in, and the opposition to them was sporadic and fragmented. My investigation soon changed into a question. Why had the Barbarians come? Why had we accepted them with so little fuss, indeed, with acclamation? In a little more than a year, I have been through the length and breadth of this city. There is going to be no revolutionary uprising against the Barbarians. Nor did they truly arrive just over a year ago. We are all Barbarians, to a greater or lesser degree - we have been for many years, and our society has been built, firmly founded, on Barbarian principles. The true Barbarians, when they came, simply pulled the covers off sores that had been there for generations. They banished the hypocrisy. They said, 'if we are Barbarians in our hearts, why shouldn't we be honest with ourselves, and behave like Barbarians, publicly and openly?' We may decide to get rid of this lot, we may decide to put the covers back on our society and appear to behave decently towards each other again. But the Barbarism will still be there, in our hearts. We talk of the time when the Barbarians came. But really, they have been here for a long time. And my philosophical enquiries under the dirty blanket of our city have only served to prove the point. Nothing will happen till people's hearts change, till they truly reject Barbaric values, and begin to live the values of community, however much it costs, instead of paying pious lip service. I can see no signs of that at all yet, only that people are getting weary of some of the Barbarians' excesses. That being so, we might just as well parade our sores in public as pick at them in private.

MARCUS: Is that really all we can look forward to?

CAPTAIN ANTONY: Look at the three of us. What will you do to save your father's patrimony: if it comes to the point? That question hasn't been asked yet. But it will be some time or other.

MARCUS: I know I like my comfort. And I realise that I can only affect detachment because I can afford to be detached.

CAPTAIN ANTONY: Indeed. At some time I too shall have to face up to the truth of what I do for a living. And Julia, of course...

MARCUS: What about Julia?

CAPTAIN ANTONY: Julia talks a great deal... but she has been having an affair with a very powerful young Barbarian businessman for nearly eight months.

*An electric pause. Marcus looks nervously towards the hidden microphones. Captain Antony calmly tops up his brandy.*

CAPTAIN ANTONY: (*Quietly*) You might as well come in now Julia. Wherever you are. Have your say.

*Julia bursts in angrily, her anger concentrated on Antony.*

JULIA: You swine... you disgusting swine....

CAPTAIN ANTONY: Did you hear it all clearly enough? Was I well placed for the mike?

JULIA: I not only heard it, Tony, it recorded quite beautifully, and will be in the hands of the necessary authorities within hours.

MARCUS: Julia...

JULIA: Shut up, Marcus, the best thing fools can do in the circumstances is to keep their mouths shut!

MARCUS: Have you been a liar and a hypocrite the whole time Julia? Deceived me right from the beginning?

CAPTAIN ANTONY: No, of course she hasn't. Only when she saw which way the wind was blowing.

JULIA: I hated them when they came here, just as much as everybody else did. It was genuine, all of it! But I'm not stupid! They're here, and they're staying, and I'm going to survive! My Barbarian is a decent enough fellow. He'll keep me in comfort, and the rest I can put up with. I don't like lost causes, and I have no intention of being a martyr to one....

> *Julia rushes out, slamming the door. After a few moments we hear her car drive off, at speed.*

MARCUS: What should we do?

CAPTAIN ANTONY: We can finish our drinks. There's no rush.

MARCUS: But Julia, she might phone, and...

CAPTAIN ANTONY: Julia will dither for a couple of hours at least, making quite sure what she is doing is in her own best interest. By which time I shall have gone. One thing however you must do.

MARCUS: What?

CAPTAIN ANTONY: You must go to the last night of **Richard the Third**, however much you might wish to be elsewhere. Your absence would be unfavourably noticed. Anyway, they tell me it's a very good production. Even without the last scene.

> *The stage floods with lurid light, and we are at the climax of Cloten's production of* **Richard the Third**. *Richard comes on, at the height of the battle. Cloten has had the brilliant idea of staging the play in the Barbarian period, so that the actors look like fifth century Goths. It is the only time we see 'traditional' Barbarian costume in the play.*

RICHARD: 'Slave, I have set my life upon a cast,

And I will stand the hazard of the die:
I think there be six Richmonds in the field,
Five have I slain today instead of him.
A horse, a horse, my kingdom for a horse!'

*Richmond enters, accompanied by four knights. Richmond engages Richard in combat, as the other four knights circle round him. The knights close in one by one, not rushing the climax. Richard is engaged by one, two, three then four knights, and fights with increasing desperation and anguish. Finally all the knights close in and stab Richard again and again. His wild cries of anguish seem sickeningly real, as he collapses onto the stage and puddles of blood run from his body. Richmond walks away, wiping his sword, as the four knights close round the fallen King, so that he cannot be seen. Marcus has been watching, horrified, from the side of the stage. As he speaks, the actor is switched for the dummy required for the end.*

MARCUS: The poor devil had no chance. Cloten had already told me that there was another knight waiting in the wings to stab him in the back if he looked like winning.

*One of the actors takes a machete from his belt and hacks off the dead King's head. The four knights rise, and we see the headless trunk, blood spurting from the neck. The knight advances downstage, brandishing the dripping severed head, which must look exactly like the actor who played the King.*

RICHMOND: 'God and your arms be praised, victorious friends;
The day is ours, the bloody dog is dead!'

*The knight brandishes the head at the audience, and stormy applause, cheers and bravos ring out from speakers all round the auditorium, so that it seems our audience and the Barbarian audience are one. The cheering fades as the actors take their delighted bows, so that Marcus' voice can be clearly heard over the ovation.*

MARCUS: The whole evening was a tremendous success for Adrian and Cloten. The blood on the stage was real at last, and genuine Barbarians will always pay good money for that kind of entertainment.

*The lights fade on Marcus as the applause becomes even louder. The actors finish taking their bows, and run off, leaving the headless trunk still centre stage, spewing blood. A pool of light comes up on Marcus, on a different part of the stage. As he speaks, lights come on to suggest a shadowy river bank, the darkness beneath a bridge, warehouses. The sound of river water is heard.*

MARCUS: I saw Antony once more. He rang me up, and arranged to meet me that night, under the river bridge, by the deserted warehouses. Much too dangerous a place these days for anything but the most furtive meeting.

*The shadowy figure of Captain Antony comes on stage.*

CAPTAIN ANTONY: ( *Calling softly* ) Hallo....

MARCUS: Who is that?

CAPTAIN ANTONY: Over here. Don't be frightened.

MARCUS: Captain Antony...?

CAPTAIN ANTONY: I can't stay long..

*Cautiously, Marcus crosses to him.*

MARCUS: What do you want?

CAPTAIN ANTONY: You need not worry. This is much more dangerous for me than for you.

MARCUS: It's dangerous for everyone. The gangs run the whole of the riverside. It's a no-go area, even for the security police.

CAPTAIN ANTONY: Which makes it a degree safer for me than most other places.

MARCUS: Yes. I suppose so. But we should keep our eyes open.

CAPTAIN ANTONY: I wanted to see you once more.

MARCUS: What for?

CAPTAIN ANTONY: To give you this.

MARCUS: What is it?

CAPTAIN ANTONY: The dossier. My whole philosophical enquiry, every sheet of it. Keep it safe. Read it, and learn from it. What sort of people we are in our hearts.

MARCUS: No. I don't believe that. Original sin is the easy way.

CAPTAIN ANTONY: Then lock it in a safe somewhere, like the Book of Hell, only to be read as a terrible warning.

MARCUS: What are you going to do?

CAPTAIN ANTONY: I shall disappear for a while.

MARCUS: What about me?

CAPTAIN ANTONY: You'll be all right. Keep your head down. Then go and live quietly in that beautiful villa of yours. And maybe, when people genuinely cease being Barbarians in their hearts, we shall meet again.....

MARCUS: I hope so.

CAPTAIN ANTONY: So do I.

*They shake hands, and, for a brief moment, hold hands in silence. It is a furtive gesture of hope, but is over in a few seconds, and Captain Antony slips into the darkness and goes offstage. Marcus looks sadly after him, recognising a kind of fellow-feeling between them, then walks slowly downstage as the lights change.*

MARCUS: He went then, slipped away in the evening darkness, between the warehouses, into the riverside slums. I never saw him again. Perhaps he went abroad. Perhaps the Barbarian security men got him. Or maybe Julia's 'other people' got there first. I have no way of knowing if he is alive or not. I suspect not.... I see Julia occasionally.

*Julia moves across the stage, with her Barbarian. They present an image of utterly complacent success.*

MARCUS: She is married to her Barbarian now, and affects the bloated look and steel-blonde hair Barbarian men seem to find attractive in their wives. I understand why she did what she did, tried to get rid of both of us. We knew too much about the real life she had lived, a life she had to suppress to survive in the new life she wanted. I often wonder if she is the same person inside as I used to go to bed with. Or if that was the deception, and the vicious blonde hair is the truth.

*Adrian comes onstage, completely grey, torn, dirty trousers, bursting shoes, a long ragged coat and scarf. He looks in a dustbin and rummages for food.*

MARCUS: Adrian, of course, lost his theatre. Cloten had him out in less than nine months, and now runs the whole show. I have heard that Adrian is eking out an existence in digs somewhere, but I have no idea where.

*The lights begin to rise towards triumphant heroic splendour.*

MARCUS: Today is National Sacrifice Day, the third year running of what has now become the great festival of the year. Five of the poorest citizens of the city, of both sexes and all ages, selected from among the destitute and starving, are publicly sacrificed to the Gods of Plenty and Consumption, who are the official ikons of the state these days. It's a terrific occasion, and immensely popular, with specially composed patriotic music. Rather like the last night of the Proms, only the knives and the blood are real. But I don't go these days. I'd rather watch it on television.

*Loud, patriotic music, huge orchestras, massed choirs, cheering, banners, a triumphant apotheosis of music and light.*

# The End

# By the same author

## Stage plays

Grounds for Marriage Traverse Theatre 1967
Sisters Northcott Theatre 1968
Sam Foster Comes Home Glasgow Citizens Theatre 1969
The Roses of Eyam Northcott Theatre 1970. Samuel French 1976
The Exorcism Comedy Theatre 1975. Samuel French 1981
Out on the Lawn Watford Palace Theatre 1975
A Long March to Jerusalem Watford 1976. Samuel French 1978
The Achurch Letters Greenwich Theatre 1978
When the Actors Come Wythenshawe Theatre 1979
Brotherhood Orange Tree Theatre 1986
Daughters of Venice Waterman's Arts Centre 1991. Samuel French 1992
Retreat From Moscow New End Theatre 1993. First Writes 1994
Women of Athens Hammersmith Polish Theatre 1993
When the Barbarians Came New End Theatre 1994. First Writes 1994

## Translations

The Theban plays of Sophocles - Oedipus the King, Oedipus at Colonus, Antigone. Methuen 1986
The War plays of Euripides - Iphigenia at Aulis, The Women of Troy, Helen. Methuen 1990

## Musicals, as lyricist, with Ellen Dryden and Charles Young

The Burston Drum Waterman's Arts Centre 1988. Samuel French 1989
Summer in the Park Waterman's Arts Centre 1990. Samuel French 1991

## Poetry

Five Political Poems First Writes Publications 1994

## Autobiography

Days of Vision Methuen 1986

**When the Barbarians Came** began with Cavafy's poem, *Waiting for the Barbarians*, which, in 1989, sparked off my own poem, *Under the Barbarians*.

In 1991, while the poem was still unfinished, it became a radio play, with its present title, broadcast by the BBC in January 1992.

Shortly after the transmission, an amateur company, THE EDGE, asked permission to perform the radio script at the Edinburgh Festival. They performed it well and were favourably noticed. So I decided to rewrite the play for the stage.

In response to their request, and appreciating the part they had played in its re-creation, I allowed THE EDGE to give the first amateur performance of the stage play, at the Barn Theatre, Southwold, on May 17th 1994, with the following cast:

| | |
|---|---|
| MARCUS | Ron Gamble |
| JULIA | Miranda Bowen |
| CAPTAIN ANTONY | Matthew Duggan |
| ADRIAN | Elizabeth Wood |
| AUGUSTUS | Gerry Lane |
| CLAUDIA | Vicki Wood |
| OCTAVIUS/ACTOR | Matthew Deal |
| LAVINIA | Lucille Tovey |
| TARQUIN/CLOTEN | Hedleigh Emerson |

Directed by Brian Gill

Don Taylor, November 1994

The poem, *Under the Barbarians*, is available in *Five Political Poems*, by Don Taylor, published by First Writes Publications in September 1994, price £1.50.

Don Taylor has worked as a playwright in all the media, theatre, television and radio, and has also directed nearly one hundred plays, working in all three forms.

His career began in 1960 as a drama director with BBC Television and during the sixties he did some of the most striking television productions of the age, directing the first six plays of David Mercer, with whom he had a close working relationship, described in his book, **Days of Vision**.

During the late seventies and most of the eighties he directed a series of large scale theatre classics on television, ranging from Greek Tragedies to Edward Bond, and seven original television plays of his own, including **The Testament of John**, the only television drama to be written in verse.

He continued to write poetry during this period, as well as plays for the stage, which have been presented in London and in theatres all over the country. **When the Barbarians Came** is his fifteenth stage play to achieve production, and, including radio and television plays, his fiftieth overall.

Of his published plays, **The Roses of Eyam** and **The Exorcism** are widely performed, and his Greek Tragedy translations, in verse, have become very popular and are staged all over the English speaking world.

He is married to playwright Ellen Dryden, and they have a daughter and a son.